MURDER AT LORD'S

Harry Oltheten is a well-known Dutch novelist, short story and cricket writer. His debut novel *Wit licht* (White light) was published in 2008 to rave reviews. An avid cricket book collector, he is the proud owner of more than a thousand cricket books, which includes five books written or co-authored by him.

John H. Wories is a prominent Dutch journalist and a former cricket and hockey commentator for radio and television. He was also associated with the entertainment industry for more than two decades as a member of the boards of Endemol and Talpa, two of the leading independent television production companies. John has played first-class cricket and was the manager of the Dutch cricket team.

MURDER AT LORD'S

HARRY OLTHETEN & JOHN H. WORIES

RUPA

Published by
Rupa Publications India Pvt. Ltd 2018
7/16, Ansari Road, Daryaganj
New Delhi 110002

Sales Centres:
Allahabad Bengaluru Chennai
Hyderabad Jaipur Kathmandu
Kolkata Mumbai

Copyright © Harry Oltheten & John H. Wories 2018
Translated by Nelleke Bezems

ISBN: 978-81-291-5163-6

First impression 2018

10 9 8 7 6 5 4 3 2 1

The moral right of the author has been asserted.

Printed in India by Thomson Press India Ltd. Faridabad

I am prepared to die, but there is no cause for which I am prepared to kill.
The human voice can never reach the distance
that is covered by the small voice of conscience.

—MAHATMA GANDHI

Thanks 4 all
the laughs on
and off the
golf course!!

J. J.

July 2019

Contents

Mohammed / 78

Michael / 82

Dick / 86

Vinoo / 92

Mohammed / 95

Michael / 98

Tony / 102

Dick / 107

Vinoo / 112

Allan / 115

Mohammed / 121

Dick / 125

Allan / 131

Michael / 135

Vinoo / 139

Dick / 143

Mohammed / 147

Tony / 153

Michael / 157

Allan / 162

Vinoo / 167

Dick / 172

Mohammed / 177

Tony / 182

Allan / 187

Michael / 192

Vinoo / 197

Dick / 202

Tony / 207

Dramatis personae

Vinoo Ramji

An Indian boy who, inspired by his grandfather, is obsessed with cricket from a very young age. With a height of 5 feet and 3 inches, he is as short as his great hero Sachin Tendulkar. He turns into a 'Boy Wonder' who enters the Indian team when he is virtually still a child. His marriage with Aasia—a Bollywood star loved by the entire male population of India—does not bring him happiness, mainly because he is still deeply in love with his childhood sweetheart, Deepika, with whom he ends up having a secret affair. In the corrupt world of cricket, the betting syndicates regard him as a big fish they would love to haul in. Will Vinoo's integrity prove fatal to him?

Allan Moorcombe

The English cricket team's coach. After a Test match in the West Indies, he is manhandled by a thug in his hotel room. He is accused by one of the betting syndicates of not complying with their urgent request to leave his star players out of the team so the victory could go to the weak West Indians. Since then, there is a constant threat. Allan is married to Valerie, a homebody. Urged by a new neighbour, she transforms herself into a fashionable lady—a metamorphosis Allan finds somewhat disquieting.

Dick Anthony

The young, ambitious reporter of *The Northern Chronicle*, a small-town newspaper in Yorkshire. Although marked by a harelip, he possesses immense confidence which comes in handy when chasing local and provincial scoops. Dick is obsessed with cricket and is invited by his best friend Phil to visit Lord's, the holy ground of cricket. This trip to London has enormous consequences and ends up with Dick being involved in a major cricket scandal. His family comprises his wife Julie, a beauty who has chosen him over a host of admirers, and his little sons, Ben, Harry and Owen.

Mohammed Musa

A Pakistani hitman who has left a trail of dead bodies in the streets of Karachi. After his umpteenth job, his boss tells him to take it easy for a while. His new 'job' consists of grooming and bribing cricketers to play the game of corruption. He is sent to London for the World Cup where he sets to work. A visit to the Lord's pharmacy proves to be pivotal.

Michael Cookson

The captain of the English cricket team, throughout his life, has been the quintessential golden boy. Luck seems to be his constant companion until he is rejected by Muriel—an enigmatic beauty—who proves to be unattainable. He takes to drinking and gambling. Due to his impulsive nature, his life spirals downwards.

Tony Abbott

The physiotherapist of the English cricket team and the ultimate confidant of many players. He is a taciturn, giant of a man and in that respect, the complete opposite of his friend, the garrulous Allan Moorcombe. His disturbed relationship with his ex-wife Helen is often the topic of conversation with Michael who is still haunted by his humiliating experience with Muriel. When Michael gets into trouble, he turns to Tony for a huge favour. But things only go from bad to worse.

Prologue

'After you were born, I knew immediately I would call you Adhira. Adhira—the name of lightning. You came like a flash.' He added, 'Just like taking a shit! Those were your mother's exact words. Of course I wasn't in the room at the time. Delivering babies is women's work. You were a lovely baby, with a full head of beautiful black hair. Yes, you could have done with a haircut right away. I was so proud.'

'And you still are, aren't you?' Adhira said mischievously, certain as she was of a positive reaction. Her father was everything to her. But she had been very disappointed when he had done nothing to protect her. Her forced marriage to Jagat—a man almost half a century older—had stung her like a scorpion. 'Jagat will tame you,' her mother had said. 'He is old and wise and he'll know how to keep you in line.' No more dates by the high tree in the village square, no more rides on her boyfriend Ajay's scooter. 'You act like a hooker,' her mother would often say. 'You're much too easy, handing out favours.'

Jagat was not just old, he was ugly too. Repulsively ugly. Two of his front teeth were missing and heavy smoking had coloured his remaining teeth dirty-yellow; his foul breath could kill a bear. Adhira had hoped that, given his advanced age, he would leave her alone. But every night he would pounce on her in an attempt to squeeze his flaccid member into her. It was pathetic.

She could only think of Ajay. That was when she started meeting him secretly. She wanted a real man, not a foul-smelling old wreck. After a month she was pregnant. Seventeen, married to an impotent man and pregnant. 'You see,' her mother said, 'Jagat is still very capable.' Jagat said nothing. As if to prove himself, he made an ultimate attempt to achieve an ejaculation shortly after her pregnancy was announced, but he was too weak. A few days later, a heart attack finally killed him.

After her husband's death, she moved back in with her parents. Her mother avoided her, because she held her daughter responsible for Jagat's death. 'I wouldn't be surprised if you poisoned him,' she said on one of the very few occasions they spoke. 'I know you wanted to get rid of him.' Adhira ignored her. Her father was more than enough for her; he spoiled her rotten. Even after several months, she barely showed a bump. Sometimes she wondered if it was all a dream, but then the kicking in her belly told her otherwise. After nine months now, she was anxiously awaiting the big moment.

She knew a baby could be late, but three weeks! Survinda, the midwife, did not panic. 'The later the arrival, the more beautiful the child will be,' she said with a reassuring smile. 'Don't be afraid. Trust me.'

When the contractions started, Adhira was convinced that she was going to bear a giant. But when Vinoo finally appeared, he turned out to be a wrinkled little creature, weighing barely five pounds. 'Everything will be all right,' Survinda said. 'Maybe he'll get big later.' But Vinoo stayed small—so small that Adhira, who was superstitious, consulted a fortune teller to confirm that all was well with her little darling.

The fortune teller could have easily doubled as Jagat's

twin although he missed all his teeth and his breath was even more repellent. 'He is destined for greatness,' he said after many calculations and hand-readings. And then, he added, 'But it's uncertain if this star will shine for long.'

1

Vinoo

AFTER THE SPRINT TO his grandfather's house, little Vinoo Ramji was always so exhausted that he would stop at the front door, resting his hands on his scabby knees. It was never for long, because he knew that his hero was waiting anxiously for his arrival. His grandfather's lemonade was the sweetest Vinoo had ever tasted. And he always prepared a lot of lemonade so that his grandson never had to be without a drink while listening to his exciting stories. 'He is destroying those nice teeth of yours,' Adhira, Vinoo's mother, always said. 'That sticky stuff will eat up that shining white enamel.'

Many of his grandfather's stories were about how poor they had been in the past, so poor that in his youth he had been a ragged little scarecrow. 'You could count my ribs,' he'd say. 'A bag of bones, that's what I used to be.' This seemed beyond belief now, because the man sitting opposite Vinoo in a beautifully carved chair, in which absolutely nobody else was allowed to sit, was anything but little. He was over six feet tall and despite his advanced age, he was still in magnificent shape. What fascinated Vinoo most were his steely grey, almost continuous eyebrows, grown to an impressive size, with the tails pointed neatly upwards as if he was the devil incarnate. He would often be seen twirling them around his fingers.

He had been quite a good cricketer himself, had even made it to the Indian Test team once, but he hardly spoke about his own career. And when he did, he confined himself to a few sparse comments. 'Yes, I once made a century before lunch with a dozen sixes and yes, I took the wickets of the first three batsmen for nought with my treacherous leg breaks, but ah well, those were exceptions.' 'False modesty,' Vinoo's mother used to say, laughing. 'Actually, he is as proud as a peacock of his achievements and he is very sorry he had to stop when he was only thirty years old because of a nagging back injury.'

False modesty or not, for Vinoo, his grandfather was his hero. Whenever he narrated fascinating stories about C.K. Nayadu, the patriarch of Indian cricket, and the 'Little Master', Sachin Tendulkar, it filled him with anticipation. Although he knew both stories by heart, he was always excited for the few minutes of pure pleasure.

Like always, getting ready for his performance, his grandfather leaned towards him as if he wanted to involve Vinoo in a conspiracy only they knew about. And then, he began:

'The first of December of 1926 was an ordinary working day, but nobody in Bombay contemplated doing anything useful. After all, the English MCC cricketers were in town. Contrary to expectations, the Indian climate and food did not have any victims. So much the better, for there were only thirteen of them. Jack Hobbs, Herbert Sutcliffe, Frank Woolley and Fred Root,'—Vinoo's grandfather always pronounced their names as if he was savouring some delicious dish—'were not part of the team, but those who were, needed to be strong enough to defeat the Indian team they were playing against. Captain Arthur Gilligan thought they were as strong as reported in every newspaper, and he was proven right. They had the Indian team in their pockets. Until Bombay, that is.'

Having gotten that far in the story, Grandfather lit a cigarette as always, despite his wife having strictly forbidden him because of his asthma. He was particularly fond of Players, the packet with the sea dog, which Vinoo was always instructed to secretly buy for him. After a few deep drags, Grandfather lowered his voice. 'The first day was dominated by Maurice "Chubby" Tate. The Indians were petrified; they just couldn't cope with his swing and serve. Admittedly, they were not top-quality. But that didn't discourage the people of Bombay. There were twenty thousand of them and my friend Ganish and I were there too. But we weren't in the stadium. We couldn't afford a ticket. We had a seat high up on a dead tree from where we could just see the pitch, through the opening between two stands. It was from there that we saw how Guy Searle, the dreaded hard hitter, scored 130 in ninety minutes, including a six, which shattered a window in the pavilion.

'The next day, we were all set. The sun was burning holes in the ground and there was not a gust of wind. Our headscarves were of no use at all against the scorching heat and we were perspiring like pigs. I can still remember the thick beads of sweat on my friend's forehead. Our expectations were not high. The 363 runs the English had scored on the first day seemed completely beyond our reach. Ganish and I were just about to lower ourselves to the ground when a booming sound came wafting out of the stadium. "Nayadu!" I heard my friend's shout above the noise. "C.K. Nayadu." And there he was. Bolt upright, he strode into the arena, as if he had swallowed a broomstick. He was my God; he was the God of all Indians.

'The third ball he received made an immense arc and landed on the roof of the pavilion. The crowd went wild. They knew they were about to witness something big. In no time, Nayudu had a score of 33. But that wasn't enough. We demanded more and he understood. He dashed forward, misjudged the ball completely and presented bowler Ewart Astill with a sitter. For a split second, it was absolutely quiet. But our fear was unfounded, because Astill, blinded by the sun, let the ball slip through his fingers. I am sure the whole town must have heard the enormous sighs of relief from the stadium.'

At that point in the story, Grandfather always paused for yet another cigarette, inhaling the smoke with even more pleasure than the first. Vinoo knew he was getting ready for the grand finale. That he knew the outcome never bothered him.

'I knew that Ganish had to relieve himself. "After the next six, I really have to go," he shouted. He didn't have to wait long. Nayadu was beginning to taste success. Another ball flashed from his bat, took to the air and disappeared into the white heat of the sun. I only saw it again when it was too late, when it hit Ganish's temple with a sledgehammer's blow. My friend looked at me wide-eyed. Then, he slowly let go of the trunk of the tree he had been clinging to. From my high seat, I could see how his neck snapped. I almost said "heard", but of course that was not possible. The loud cheers of the public were too deafening for that. Naturally, I got down as fast as I could but there was nothing I could do. He was dead. As dead as a doornail.'

Every single time Grandfather reached the end of his story, Vinoo saw tears in his beautiful, brown eyes. After a few seconds, he'd brush them away, looking a bit embarrassed. 'Nayadu scored a 153. The match ended in a draw and the Indians celebrated this as a victory, but I only heard that after the cremation during which I felt so miserable that the whole ceremony passed me by completely.'

Vinoo knew that after this ending there was more to come. His grandfather always saved the best for last. He very carefully pushed a tape into an antiquated video. 'Look at Sachin,' he said. 'Look at Sachin and enjoy yourself.' And that was precisely what Vinoo did, especially when he saw how a boy of just seventeen snatched the ball from just above the grass after a long dash. '1 July 1990. Lord's was on fire. Never forget that date. Promise me that.' As always, his grandfather was very emotional. Vinoo nodded respectfully. He knew he had witnessed the birth of a genius in that video.

When, after many glasses of lemonade, he would run home on his short legs, he would imagine he was the Little Master. He, the shortest in his class, felt a kinship with Sachin, who, with his five feet three inches—a fact always stressed by his grandfather—had actually become the best cricket player in the world. How many times he had imitated his hero's catch he didn't know, but what he did know for sure was that one day he would do it for real.

2

Allan

ALLAN MOORCOMBE, THE ENGLISH cricket team's coach, loved his food hot and spicy. Everybody knew that because he was always bragging about his capacity to eat the hottest dishes. He often placed bets with a member of the touring cricket team regarding who could eat the hottest curry. While his opponents, sweating profusely, would battle through their food, he never showed any discomfort—watching them, as cool as a cucumber.

But now he had apparently gone too far with his (Very) Spicy Chicken Vindaloo. Ed Morrison—not only an excellent batsman but also the proud owner of an iron stomach—was observing him with a smile on his face, certain of his victory. Allan couldn't care less. At dinner, while the cricketers were bandying about their scurrilous jokes, sharp pains in his belly announced disaster. Just after dessert—a chocolate coconut cake the rest of the men could not get enough of—he made a dash for the toilet where his guts seemed to explode. Back at the table, he was soon the butt of their childish jokes. 'You big sissy! Only porridge for you tomorrow!' He didn't rise to their bait. He was longing for the quiet of his room, where in about an hour, Taniyah would pay him a visit.

The awful thought that he would have the runs while he was

in his favourite position on top of her sent a shiver down his spine. Taniyah had made his stay in Barbados worthwhile. The rest of the tour had been a disaster. The West Indies were not the champions they once were and losing against such a weak team, even though it was in only one of the three Tests, was a downright disgrace. With an anxious grimace, he stood up and took his leave from his men. 'See you tomorrow at nine.' Tony Abbott, the physiotherapist of the team, nodded. He was a taciturn man—for him, every word counted.

In Room No. 11, it was freezing, thanks to a roaring air conditioner—not quite the right atmosphere for the things to come. Shivering with cold and nausea, he switched it off, flopped down on the bed and tried to relax. To be sure, he went to the toilet just before Taniyah's expected arrival, but the result was negligible—only a bit of slime.

He felt a fleeting guilt about his escapades. Valerie did not deserve this. Always in her unattractive oversized apron, she 'held the fort' in London, as she always called it. He had married her when he was twenty and she was nineteen. A shotgun wedding. Back then, she had made him feel like the real He-Man. Her loud, shrill laughter at the jokes he fired at her had bolstered his ego and it hadn't bothered her that he was almost as short as she was. And yet, quite soon after their marriage, he cheated on her for the first time.

He didn't feel much remorse and Valerie seemed to be completely unaware. She had guided their twins through an awkward puberty all on her own and now Jimmy was a student at Cambridge and Melanie studied at Durham, both doing unexpectedly well. Enjoying a moment of paternal pride he settled on the bed, looking forward to the steaming sex he had gotten to know so well lately, incomparable to the occasional sex he had with Valerie.

The knock on the door sounded more forceful than usual. Allan smiled, happy that she shared his anticipation. A fifty-year-old sharing a bed with a twenty-year-old; be it at a price—what could be nicer? Of all the prostitutes he had slept with on his tours, she was by far the most attractive. And she didn't seem to do it for the money.

Another knock on the door, even more forceful than the first. He straightened his shirt, sucked in his stomach and walked to the door. He was looking forward to their greeting ritual—even before she would cross the threshold, she would jump into his arms and fasten her legs around his waist. It played hell with his oncoming hernia, but he always managed to hide that this apparent sign of affection gave him an excruciating backache.

What came next always taxed him to the utmost. Taniyah, tried and tested in her trade, would drag him through an exhausting course of assault which often made him fear for his life. *The respected English coach Allan Moorcombe dies in the arms of a whore.* The newspapers would lap it up! But Valerie and the children would be crushed, although he wasn't so sure about Jimmy, his eldest.

The door stuck a little, so when it gave way after a fierce pull, he almost fell over backwards into the room. He regained his balance with difficulty. 'Your sweetheart can't make it tonight,' said the man in the doorway whose voice sounded muffled because of the balaclava he was wearing. 'She loves you very much, but sorry, she had a hotter date. With a twenty-year-old, I believe. But maybe a little rest will do you some good. She told me you lack stamina.' He closed the door behind him and pushed Allan with the barrel of his gun pointing at him.

'A Heckler & Koch,' said the man, who had noticed Allan's fixed stare. 'With a silencer, of course. We don't want to alarm the neighbours. Perhaps they're oversensitive. That seems to be a common ailment nowadays.' He drove the weapon against Allan's chest and pushed his victim towards the wall. 'I think we should have a brief but probing conversation,' he said. 'I firmly believed that you would take last week's telephone call seriously. You do remember, don't you?'

Allan's brain wasn't working properly, as if it was dipped in molasses. He was seized by a crippling fear. His bowels were fancying another go and pushed a thin stream towards his sphincter which was about to give up. 'No way,' he thought, squeezing his buttocks as hard as he could. 'No way, not now.'

'Well?' said the man. 'Do you need a reminder?' With a fierce blow his fist landed just below Allan's diaphragm. 'That is the solar plexus,' he said. 'Always extremely painful.' But Allan had stopped listening. Not only had a sharp pain gripped his body, he could also smell the ooze running down his legs. 'Never mind,' said the man. 'That's the problem with you sissies. You're too easy.' Only now did Allan notice the low voice of the thug. 'You haven't answered my question,' the man said, a little impatiently. 'Well?' Allan slowly came back to his senses.

'Of course I remember,' he said. 'But I thought I was dealing with a crackpot.'

'And didn't that crackpot tell you about the consequences if you didn't follow his advice?' Allan remembered that only too well. 'Leave Hawkins and Cookson out of the team,' the man had said. 'Or else...' Not for a moment had he considered acting on that urgent advice. They would win anyway, whatever the lineup, no question about that. But Hawkins and Cookson were his stars; they couldn't be left out without reason.

'We got the result we wanted,' said the man. 'But no thanks to you. You couldn't have known that those two would go to the dressing room after a few miserable runs. Together, they could just as easily have scored a couple of hundreds, as they usually do, and then the West Indies would have had it. That it turned out okay this time doesn't mean that you don't have to obey our orders in the future. You have to pay attention, especially in six weeks' time, when the World Cup starts.'

There was a sudden gleam on the right hand of the man. 'I am left- and right-handed, ambidextrous, so to speak,' he said. 'It always comes in handy when you can use both hands.' Allan felt his face rip open when the knuckleduster hit his cheekbone. 'Don't tell anyone I was here. If you do, your children will pay for it,' were the last words he heard before losing consciousness.

3

Dick

'Enjoying the view, are you? And the spring weather?'

Dick Anthony, the young, ambitious reporter of *The Northern Chronicle* knew the man who had addressed him only too well. It was Mr Phillips, his former headmaster and an authority on local history. They had often shared this bench, gazing at the skyline of Allesford. Recently, Mr Phillips had not been stopping for their usual chat, and Dick knew the reason.

After a marriage of more than fifty years, his wife—the fattest woman Dick had ever seen—had passed away. 'My life is in pieces,' he had told Dick, on one of the rare occasions they had met. 'I'd rather be dead as well.' His loneliness was carved into his face. He had no children, which didn't surprise Dick. Overcome by compassion, he watched the old man walk away slowly. 'He's not going to last long,' he thought. 'This is killing him.'

Dick loved Allesford. Everything about the town was dear to him—the narrow river flowing right through it, its canopy of trees, the beautiful grey church from 1466 with its sturdy, squat tower, the monastery just outside the town, and of course, the untidy newsrooms of *The Northern Chronicle*, the newspaper for which he chased regional and local scoops. Dick had been inquisitive his entire life. At his primary school, one of his teachers had once called him 'Argus'. At home, he had immediately looked up the meaning of the word in his father's dictionary and the comparison with a hundred-eyed giant had made him proud, despite the gruesome end of the monster.

His latest scoop, uncovering a corruption scandal in which the biggest local building contractor and a top civil servant of the local council were involved, had earned him a pay raise and put a smile on his face. It didn't amount to much, just a drop in the ocean, and certainly not enough to take some of the weight off Julie's shoulders. She, with her part-time job as a nursery school teacher and the care of their three sons—Ben, Harry and Owen—had a lot to cope with. Julie adored him and he revelled in her adoration.

That she had fallen for him had truly surprised him. She was a well-known local beauty with a host of admirers, and he, a man with a harelip. Not that it was really visible, but still. For a while, he had hid the rough scar with a moustache. Although he had convinced himself it looked quite good on him, he soon gave up trying to hide his imperfection, certainly after Julie assured him that she loved him, with or without a moustache. 'You're my big, sexy teddy bear,' she used to say when she cuddled him. Julie was petite and hardly reached his chin. But short as she was, she was a bundle of dynamite.

One morning, when the building scandal had been at its height and he had found the tyres of his Ford Fiesta slashed to ribbons, she had almost exploded. 'Bastards, I will rip out their throats with my bare teeth.' So one Saturday afternoon, when she ran into the building contractor whom she held responsible for the crime on the High Street, she lashed out at him with her claws. He ended up with four deep, red scratches on his cheek, blood dripping on his expensive suit. But surprisingly, he did not report it.

After pondering on the bench for a while, Dick walked to the Allesford Cricket Club clubhouse on Victoria Road—his second home. At the beginning of every April, when the sun would finally emit just a smidgen of warmth, Dick would spend every minute of his spare time in the nets, refining his bowling skills. He loved the brief walk to his home ground. Every time he passed the railway overpass and reached the long wall surrounding the ground, his heart skipped a beat, just as it did now.

Dick was a fast bowler, and not a bad one either, but with the bat he was an absolute bungler. His highest score of eight, two snicks through the slips, spoke volumes. That's why everyone in his team called him 'Ted', after the New Zealand test cricketer Ted Thompson who took more wickets than he scored runs and could boast the most pairs in cricket history. The evening after Dick had almost made 10 runs, he and his team had celebrated this feat boisterously, after which he had tottered home drunk as a skunk. That in the same match he had taken 4 for 32, no one remembered.

Opening the door of the dressing room, Dick involuntarily thought of Joe, and of the innumerable times the two of them had changed into their cricket whites in this same room. He still missed him every day. His elder brother had been his superior in almost everything. He had been even taller than Dick who measured a respectable 6.3.

Joe had possessed an uncanny resemblance to Rupert Brooke; he had been highly talented and an exceptional sportsman till his twenty-second birthday. Then, all of a sudden, he had started to fail his exams, had broken up with his girlfriend, had avoided the playing field and had gotten involved with the wrong crowd. The overdose that eventually killed him hadn't come as a surprise to anyone.

On the day of his funeral—2 November, All Souls' Day—the

weather had mourned too. A bleak easterly wind had blown across the graveyard and when they had left the open grave, light snow had been falling. Dick sometimes talked to Joe. His dead brother remained his support in difficult situations. His parents hadn't been able to deal with the death of their beloved son and they had died shortly after. Their death and that of his brother's still held Dick in an emotional grip.

It was a godsend that Phil Edmunds—his best friend since primary school—was with him through this. Dick always found Phil's ruddy face, his distinct paunch and his bandy legs rather endearing, but he knew only too well that his friend's somewhat comical appearance was completely misleading. Phil was the most formidable lawyer in North Yorkshire, highly in demand for his sheer tenacity and his otherworldly shrewdness.

For Dick, however, he was just a friend. *His* friend. Unlike Dick, Phil was an impressive batsman. He wasn't keen on walking, let alone running, and so, he restricted himself to fours and sixes that always came in a flurry. His top score of 130 in an hour and a half spoke for itself. 'Those guys were completely shite, a bunch of losers,' he had said later, downplaying his own achievement.

The cricket-info app on his phone kept Dick informed all the time. Even now, while changing into his cricket gear, he couldn't resist checking what was going on with his beloved sport in the rest of the world. He always had the latest news at hand: New Zealand—Sri Lanka, Australia—India; he knew all the ins and outs. Not only did he read his own newspaper *The Northern Chronicle*, but he also subscribed to *The Times* and *The Guardian*. The history of his favourite sport was a source of eternal fascination for him. His bookshelves were full of *Wisdens* and all sorts of books about the game, including the treasures he had acquired for a small fortune at an antiquarian bookshop. They were small extravagances that Julie did not begrudge him, even though they could hardly afford them.

In autumn, in winter or early spring, he would sit poring over his tablet till the early hours of the morning following events all across the globe. Recently, they had been very strange. Bizarre results, series of no-balls, incredible losses when the game was in the bag—that was the order of the day. Dick had his own ideas about the goings-on. He knew that things had not really changed since the notorious Edward Pooley had sold a match for fifty pounds in the late nineteenth century. Only today, the stakes were much higher and involved thousands if not millions of pounds. However, it did not affect his love for the king of sports, although at times, he could not help feeling uneasy when another strange incident occurred.

All day, he felt a slight nausea, but that was something he gladly put up with. Tomorrow was the big day. 'A few days away will do you a world of good,' Phil had said. 'You sink your teeth far too deep into all those trivialities. Who cares who cheats whom in Allesford? I'm taking you to Lord's. There you can see for yourself what it's all about. I'll treat you to a guided tour and afterwards we'll have dinner in some fancy restaurant.' On hearing the name of Lord's, Dick had felt a surge of pure pleasure. That was the place where in the '90s, Geoffrey Boycott, in his grey brothel-creepers, had put his car keys in the pitch for his prematch report. It was the place to be. He hadn't needed time to think. This was the chance of a lifetime. He would be mad to pass up this opportunity.

4

Mohammed

MOHAMMED MUSA HAD CHOSEN the Danubius Hotel with care. One just couldn't get any closer to Lord's. Under the blackened concrete ledge above the hotel entrance stood a porter who looked exactly like a young Emperor Hirohito, including his high hat. His curious tic did not deter his resolve. He promptly picked up Mohammed's suitcase and led the way to the hotel's reception desk. The black and grey swirly, corkscrew-like design of the carpet made Mohammed nauseous, but he kept himself steady. He gave Hirohito a two-pound tip, asked the man at the reception for the Wi-Fi code and checked in.

'Khalid Ahmed'—he still found his pseudo-name hard to get used to. He walked across the marble lobby to the elevator and made his way to his room where he felt a sense of calm take over him. The job he had to do was perfect for him. He knew he could not fail. Smiling to himself, he looked at the Bible on the bedside table; a label on the cover read, 'This book is not for sale'. As if, he thought. Here too, the decor was grotesquely tasteless. Green, black and insipid beige, all squirming for attention. He planted himself in front of the TV and watched the Discovery channel, where a man was trying to survive under extreme conditions and minimal resources. When the survivor bit into a crane fly, 'full of protein', and yellow liquid oozed between his teeth, Mohammed decided he had put up with enough. He walked to the elevator and went down to the lounge.

Mohammed's first murder still filled him with satisfaction. He was only 15 at that time, but he was determined. And of course, he had the knife, the one he had inherited from his father. It was not a big knife, but it was sharp and he carried it with him everywhere. On his deathbed his father had warned, 'Never leave the house without the knife, Mohammed. Danger is lurking around on every corner.' 'Of course,' he had replied, glowing with pride yet filled with sadness as his mother had told him that his father would never again throw a ball at the three sticks that served as a wicket in the backyard.

Cricket was his father's lifelong passion. He knew everything there was to know about it. That he instilled this passion in his son went without saying. Hours on end, they practised together in the backyard. Mohammed was the eager student his father had wished for, because Umar, three years older than Mohammed, never qualified for that role. Umar was caught in a tight squeeze at birth. 'He's nothing more than a plant,' his mother often said. 'He knows nothing, can do nothing, but I love him anyway'— something Mohammed found hard to imagine.

How could you love a huge slobbering baby who did nothing all day but shit his pants? He was never happier than when his brother was moved to an institution because he could no longer be cared for at home. His father and mother visited Umar often, but he never had to, for which he was profoundly grateful.

Just before his father fell ill, he revealed his biggest secret to Mohammed—the secret of the googly. They had just started practising this extraordinary delivery—in which the leg-break bowler's ball did not go from right to left but just the other way around—when his father became too ill to continue. Mohammed never knew what his father did for a living before stomach cancer gripped him. When he asked his parents, they remained vague. 'It's a secret. No one can know.'

This vagueness spurred on wild fantasies in which his idol, his father, was a superhero like James Bond or Superman. His father's death left a deep impression on him. Slowly, he saw the man he loved most wither away. He had always been a jolly, round and robust man, but after just a few short weeks in bed, his cheeks were hollow and there were deep crevices carved around his mouth. There was nothing left of the round belly Mohammed used to drum on while his father sang. And that was just the beginning. By the time he had breathed his last breath in their little house on a blistering hot afternoon, he had shrivelled up like a mummy.

'He wanted so much to stay with us,' his mother said. 'It was worth everything to him. That's why he fought for so long'. After his father's death, Mohammed had but one wish: to make sure his mother was okay. His father had not asked him to; it was just instinct. When they walked together in the markets of Karachi— she, with only her hands and face uncovered—he was very proud of her. She was the most beautiful and sweetest woman in the world. And it was wrong that the man in the expensive suit stared at her. The first time he noticed it might have been a coincidence, but the second, third and the fourth time, he was sure. This man wanted to steal his mother from him. This man wanted to drive a wedge between them.

One drab and listless day, his mother stayed home sick. She was often sick. Sick with grief. Near the market, Mohammed saw the man. He was standing at a fruit stall, casually squeezing and poking the fruits. Mohammed's mind was made up. Now that his mother was not with him he could act swiftly. After a few minutes, the man disappeared in the crowd but soon, Mohammed caught sight of him again. Mohammed's prey did not seem to be in the mood for shopping. He just wandered along. He followed his quarry cautiously. Just beyond the market was a labyrinth of streets and alleyways with no one in sight. It was becoming trickier to follow the man unnoticed. Mohammed hovered in a corner. He had to strike quickly.

But before he could sprint towards his victim, a hand grabbed him by the throat. 'Hey there,' he heard. 'What are you up to? I've been watching you. Where is your mother? Are you allowed out without her?' That last remark was the goad Mohammad needed. Quick as a flash, he turned around and plunged his knife into his assailant's chest. Never in his life had he seen such a bewildered expression. The man clutched his chest and sank slowly to his knees at Mohammed's feet. He quickly wiped the knife on the man's snowy white shirt and ran from the alley.

'Didn't you shop?' his mother asked when he entered the house, drenched in sweat. 'You were supposed to go to the market.' Mohammed mumbled something about running into a friend and quickly left. He had to get out of the house. Back out on the street, it felt as if everyone could see he was a killer. It felt as if it was inscribed on his forehead, that he had killed a man who probably meant no harm, that he had stabbed him in the chest, straight through his heart.

But that was just the prelude. A few years later, working for Javed Hussain, killing became his day job. His way up the ladder was steep; he was ruthless, his methods creative. Poison, rope or gun, he didn't care. After his grand masterpiece—the murder of a rival gang boss—Hussain allowed him to take it a bit easy. He didn't have to kill anymore, he just had to master the art of persuasion.

And he did. He was the man who had to persuade cricket players to break all the rules of the game. He knew exactly how to do that. He was the best, and that was why he was in London.

He sat at the bar, ordered a tonic and looked around. On the way to the lounge he had passed the Barrington and Grace Suite but this, the bar, was really it. He gazed at the black and white photographs of Sunil Gavaskar, Don Bradman, and Ian Botham with his impressive mullet blowing in the wind. He could not suppress a smile. This hotel breathed cricket. Of course he knew that the English Test team stayed here and who he needed to 'persuade'. He had done his homework. After a few minutes he left the bar and went outside. He turned the corner and stood face-to-face with the wall that surrounded his new area of business. 'Hello Lord's, here I come,' he murmured contentedly as he lit a strong Pakistani cigarette, without filter. He would have to be frugal; he only had a few packs left.

5

Michael

'MAY I TAKE YOUR coat, Mr Cookson?' Although irritated by the man's servility, the English cricket teams' captain managed a curt 'yes'. He was perspiring slightly. 'Stress,' he thought. A few shots of scotch to steady his nerves before he hit the poker tables couldn't hurt. 'Sports and alcohol do not mix,' his father had always told him—an advice he never heeded. After all, he was as strong as an ox; his resilient constitution never failed him. Even after a boozy night in the town, he would be fit as a fiddle the next morning. The first sip was a direct hit. Even though he knew it was the second glass that usually put him at the top of his game, that first one instantly made him feel stronger. He motioned to the bartender and prepared for a big night.

Everyone considered Michael Cookson the 'golden boy', and they weren't just referring to his golden crop of hair. Till he was 25, everything had come easy to him—unlike for his twin brother Julian, who was older than him by half an hour. From a very young age, and much to the dismay of his parents, Julian had been a contentious child. Even the unconventional art school, which he eventually attended, didn't know what to do with him. These days he kept himself afloat by selling Anselm Kiefer-like paintings. He didn't sell much, but that didn't seem to bother him. Julian was the black sheep of the family and was rarely mentioned. But Michael kept in contact with him and even found himself jealous of his brother's happy-go-lucky lifestyle—a stark contrast to his own.

That everything had seemingly been easy for Michael was largely thanks to his father, a respected heart surgeon with several pioneering surgeries to his name. He had made sure Michael was accepted by Eton and again by Cambridge. His academic performance had been far from brilliant—a measly third division in English was all he could boast of—but no one had cared, least of all his father. He often suspected his old man had bribed the professor who had evaluated his thesis, something he never would have done for Julian.

Michael was an athlete who excelled at all kinds of sport. His exceptional performances could often be witnessed at Fenner's university cricket ground in Cambridge. He went all out for the matches against their arch rival Oxford where he chose to showcase his most memorable performances. Once he scored 150 runs, including 20 sixes that sailed right out of the field. That Middlesex scooped him up was no surprise and that he shot through to the English Test team was unavoidable. He was destined for greatness.

With his looks it was no wonder he was a ladies' man. They fell for him in droves. In Cambridge, there were rumours about the fantastic size of his penis and the amazing things he could do with it. No, he could not lose with the ladies. Then Muriel Clark appeared in his life; she was a special girl. It was whispered that her mother was the illegitimate child of Alec Atkinson—the Labour Party politician who died so suddenly in 1967 that foul play was suspected.

Even though she was not nearly as pretty as all his previous girlfriends, Muriel was the first woman for whom he really had to make an effort. There was something about her strangely tilted eyes and Modigliani-like face that he found irresistible. He had to have her, forget the rest. In his dreams, he ripped her clothes off and fucked her for hours, until she begged for mercy. He got her phone number from her friend—one of his conquests—and called her numerous times for a date—unsuccessfully. He tried all his charming tricks, but still ended up being called a shallow dickhead at a party. At that moment something cruel awoke in him. She would pay for this. How dare she reject him—the star Test player Michael Cookson.

One boozy night at 'The Mitre', he watched her from the corner of his eye as she left the pub alone and followed her. He assumed she heard his footsteps following her; she *had* to hear him—that was the plan. He wanted to teach her a lesson; he wanted to scare the daylights out of her. But she did not flinch, not once did she look back. Near her college, Newnham, he grabbed her from behind. 'You're mine,' he murmured, half-drunk. 'You know you're the only one for me.' The sharp pain that shot through his balls came out of nowhere. No one had told him that Muriel was a karate expert—second Dan.

He tried to put her out of his mind, but her memory kept nagging him, even after Carine Stewart—a medical student and renowned beauty queen known for her fiery red hair and stunning figure—fell for his charms. She left her studies midway and went to London with him where they moved in together near Kensington Gardens. But Muriel had changed him. He became irritable. Even becoming captain of the English Test team gave him little pleasure. It certainly stroked his colossal ego, but the thrill was short-lived. However, there was one good thing about this—there was plenty of money from his contracts and advertising deals. He made a commercial promoting men's hair loss shampoo, in which he rose like Venus—not from the sea, but from a bubble bath while massaging the wonder-drug in his hair and flaunting his impressive torso.

Accustomed as he was to continuous praise and adulation, the recent criticism was new to him. The tour to the West Indies had finally closed on a win, but the big loss in the last Test had caused an uproar with the British sports journalists. How could they lose against such a washed-out team? Michael even had to answer to *News at Ten*. He had charmed his way through the interview, but the comments in the next day's papers were merciless—'glib' they called him—'too sleek', 'Teflon Michael'. All this had driven him straight to the place where he felt most at home these days—the casino. He loved the pomp and circumstance, the exquisite lobster they served, but most of all, he loved the poker table. It didn't bother him that he had recently lost so much at the table—after all, he had plenty.

6

Vinoo

Master colah adored the young Vinoo Ramji. Vinoo was exceptional—excellent in the classroom and unbeatable on the sports field. He himself had not been much of a cricketer, but as a coach, no one was his equal. After school, he often practised with Vinoo in the schoolyard, polishing the young diamond in the rough. He soon realized that bowling was not Vinoo's forte, his stubby little fingers were just too short. But as a batsman, he was more than promising. Vinoo, small as he was, could hit a ball—hard, fast and far.

His classmates, perhaps unconsciously realizing they were watching a star batsman in the making, were only too happy to fetch the balls for him. Thanks to Vinoo, his school was unbeatable in regional competitions. High scores were the standard. In the back of his mind, Vinoo was haunted by the magical number 501. His grandfather had told him about the West Indian phenomenon Brian Lara who in 1994 had scored 501 runs for his county Warwickshire in a match against Durham. 'And he was not out,' Grandfather always said with sparkling eyes. This was Vinoo's ambition. And he achieved it.

Against a neighbouring school with a pretty good cricket team, he batted for seven gruelling hours and made 502 runs before he was clean bowled by a full toss which was meant to go for a six. 'Not bad,' his grandfather said, 'but "not out" would have been better.' Vinoo was taken aback by his grandfather's remark, but when he saw the sparkle in his hero's eyes, he overflowed with pride. For a moment, he deemed himself invincible.

The ball that hit him in the eye brought him back to reality— both feet firmly on the ground. 'You're lucky,' the doctor said. 'This could have ended far worse.' Vinoo nodded guiltily. Of course he should have dodged the beamer. Someone with his talent for speed should have avoided it. He had just been too arrogant; too convinced of the incompetence of his opponent. He had never been in such wild panic. The blindness that hit him had made him run around frantically in pure fear. His coach and grandfather had to manhandle him before they could race him to the hospital in Master Colah's old Suzuki. It took three days before he regained a blurry sight in his left eye and much longer before his vision was clear again.

'It is a lesson,' his grandfather, who came to visit every day, said. 'Pride comes before a fall. It could have ended horribly. You could have been blinded' In the first match after his injury, Vinoo was not his old self. It took him more than an hour for 11 stolen singles. Only when he noticed his grandfather's impatient waving did he kick it up a notch. The 58 runs he eventually scored were a bit beneath his dignity, but under the circumstances, he was reasonably happy.

His extraordinary talent did not go unnoticed and Vinoo was selected for a trial. Players and staff met in Mumbai, close to Taloja, Vinoo's village—a barren and desolate place. It was a hot day and Vinoo almost lost consciousness standing at the wicket, but he still managed to make a century without a single mistake. 'We're impressed,' said the coach of the Indian cricket league. 'You're going to go far.'

After this, to calm himself down, Vinoo took an evening stroll near his hotel. On Mahatma Gandhi Road, he noticed a beautiful doorway which appeared to lead to a cricket ground. The sign above read 'Bombay Gymkhana'. Timidly, he went inside and saw luxury like he had never seen before. Men, lounging in wicker armchairs, were watching a match between two pot-bellied teams. Vinoo was just about to sit down when he heard someone roar: 'How dare you come in here! This is for members only, not for brats like you.' The screaming man was beside himself with rage. 'Get out! Now!'

Vinoo hardly dared to look up. The large man he had apparently offended looked as if he was about to explode, as if he had never been so insulted. Vinoo worried he would get a kick in his backside, but he reached the street unharmed. He was shaking all over and only calmed down as he reached the ground where the trials were happening.

After that, things really took off. The Mumbai Indians were excited by this small wonder boy who scored run after run. At 16, he made his entrance into the IPL and although he only scored 17 runs in his first game, four fours and one single, they had faith in him, and rightly so. In a thrilling match against Royal Challengers Bangalore, he came in at five and immediately launched a six which ended high in the stands. The audience was ecstatic.

During the rest of the innings, he was reckless, but lucky. His last and deciding six soared narrowly a metre above the grass, but nevertheless made the boundary. A star was born, but a star who proved fallible in the next match.

It was sink or swim against the Kolkata Night Riders. Vinoo felt every nerve ending in his body tingle with tension. The tremors in his arms and legs were a sure sign of how much was at stake. He wished he was a man of steel, immune to the anxiety that gripped him. He somehow wanted to tip the stakes in favour of his team, to chalk up the victory to his name. With the last man from Kolkata at the wicket, they needed five more runs in the final ball. The tail ender who, up until then, had only played with air—drawing sympathy from the spectators—finally made contact.

The ball launched in the air and sailed in Vinoo's direction who cupped his hands for an easy catch just inside the boundary. This was his moment of glory, he was sure of it. But the ball suddenly dropped faster than expected and disappeared from his field of vision. By the disappointed howl of the spectators he knew he had missed his great opportunity. Because of his previous performance, the press spared him; but for a while the bright shining star seemed dim.

Sachin Tendulkar's biography was his favourite book. He spent endless hours reading it and it taught him a lot. He often read it aloud to his girlfriend Deepika, whom he was madly in love with. Vinoo was not of high birth; Deepika came from even more humble beginnings. 'Surely you can do better,' Deepika often said, but that just made Vinoo love her more. He would never leave Deepika. He knew that for sure.

7

Tony

'Don't tell anybody,' James Hawkins, one of England's most famous Test players said. He didn't really expect a reply, it was more of a comment. He knew he could trust his physiotherapist Tony Abbott. The entire English team trusted Tony. Tony knew all the players in his care, and he knew their innermost thoughts and feelings. He was a confidant to most. That's why James told him. He had to tell someone. Tony thought the Pakistani, who had approached James in the hotel was probably harmless; he most likely just wanted to chat with the famous cricketer—a few comments about the weather, a random question about the team's lineup. But still, something was not quite right. The invitation to dinner was a just a bit too odd.

Tony's mother often told the story of how he did not utter a single word before the age of three. Not even the words 'mommy' or 'daddy', although why he never said 'daddy' was understandable. When his father had learned of the pregnancy, he had taken off as fast as he could. Growing up, Tony saw his father every fortnight. Despite the fact that his father had treated his mother so despicably, Tony liked the man who took him, as a kind of mascot, to the pub on Saturdays where his father invariably got outrageously drunk.

He developed a symbiotic relationship with his mother. They were always together.

When Tony was about seven years old, his mother met Ken Peterson, a man twenty years her senior, who gave her the stability she needed. Tony, however, decided the relationship was unacceptable and stopped talking. Fortunately, one of his teachers, Mr Bell, saw what was troubling him and drew him out of his silence. As if compensating for his lack of speech, Tony just grew. By the time he was fifteen years old, he was over 6.5. His mother insisted he joined the best basketball club in the city. He had a natural aptitude and the club was eager to have him. But he did not join the club; his interest lay elsewhere.

For as long as he could remember, he had been fascinated by the men in white, flaunting their cricket skills on TV. He soaked up Richie Benaud's commentary and was fascinated with his face—a mass of wrinkles. He relished Brian Johnston's giggles as he made another wisecrack. When Phil Tufnell was up, Tony was glued to the TV. Phil's boyish face and magical spin balls fascinated him endlessly. So, with his first bowling efforts on the municipal lawn in front of his house, Tony did not imagine running a great distance like the dreaded West Indians from long ago. No, a few steps were enough. 'The master of the inscrutable effect,' as Phil commentated—that's what he wanted to be.

It was not a memorable career. He barely made it to the second eleven of Nottinghamshire. And although his dream to make it internationally did not come true, he didn't really mind. He was a successful and valued physiotherapist now and felt at home with his team. He had made it to the premier league as a physiotherapist, and then, thanks to his magical hands, the English Test team.

Coach Allan Moorcombe, in every way his opposite, became his best friend. Tony was more than 6.5; Allan barely 5.7. Tony was wiry, almost skinny; Allan was round and plump, but the biggest contrast was that Tony kept his silence and Allan was loose-lipped and indiscrete. His chattiness and many indiscretions were usually forgiven—'just typical Allan'. In Barbados, however, he went too far, even needing medical attention. 'Slipped in the bathtub,' was his curt explanation the next morning, 'bad landing on the edge.' Ten stitches was the result and they did not heal well. 'Another beauty mark,' Allan quipped unconvincingly, pointing to the rough scar on his cheek.

The next World Cup would be Tony's biggest test to date. All his men were fit but that could change overnight. He remembered the wave of injuries a few years ago all too well. Two torn ligaments, a ruined hamstring, a damaged shoulder and a burnout had left them vulnerable. As James jumped sprightly off the massage table, Tony shivered at the thought, 'That must not happen again.' All of England held her breath. Was it not Admiral Horatio Nelson, who had said 'England expects every man to do his duty'? It was now truer than ever.

8

Allan

A␣ᴌᴌᴀɴ ᴡᴀs ᴛᴀᴋᴇɴ ᴀʙᴀᴄᴋ after seeing the makeover. Where was the woman he had left behind in their big house more than six weeks ago? Where was the big apron? And the long hand-knitted sweater? He had never seen her in a short dress nor had he seen her hair so bouncy and glamorous—a long shot from the tight perm he was used to. 'How do you like it?' she asked, taking on a cheeky pose as he walked through the door. 'Very nice,' he murmured. 'Incredibly nice.' But he really didn't know how to react.

He had never thought that Valerie was a particularly attractive woman. Sure, he had lusted after her when he was young, but that was more because she was easier to get than the other girls he had dated. 'So, the newspapers were quite nasty.' Allan felt a familiar twinge. Some things never change. She always knew how to say the wrong thing at the wrong time. And there was always that bitter undertone. The phone in his pocket vibrated. He gently pushed Valerie aside, and walked into the kitchen, closing the door behind him.

'Home sweet home,' he heard, 'there's no place like home. But watch your little wife; she's wilder than you think. And remember our last conversation. I know you love your kids; paternal love, very commendable.' Before Allan could answer, the connection was broken.

'That scar suits you,' Valerie said as he walked back into the hall. 'It makes you look tough.' Allan felt a slight nausea creep over him and longed for his first drink. The promotional tour in the United States after that disaster in the West Indies had exhausted him. The Americans regarded cricket as 'baseball on valium,' as the tragic Robin Williams had once joked. The days when baseball heroes like Babe Ruth entertained cricket legends like Donald Bradman in a private box in the New York Yankees Stadium were long gone.

₩

'Hello Allan!' Brian Jameson's slap on his shoulder was, as usual, just a bit too friendly. Brian—the chairman of the English Cricket Board—and Alan had agreed to meet on the terrace of 'The Lord's Tavern' next to the stadium for an 'informal chat', as Brian put it. After the obligatory niceties about their spouses and children and Allan explaining his new scar, Brian abruptly came to the point. 'That last Test was rubbish! Hawkins and Cookson back in the clubhouse for virtually nothing. Unprecedented. Those West Indians are useless. You should beat them by innings—we can't settle for less. Are you sure those stars of yours are on the up-and-up? No funny business going on?'

Allan thought about the man with the dark voice and instinctively touched his scar. Their Lord's Beef Burgers were served, cutting the conversation short. Eating the burgers was a challenge. With malicious pleasure, Allan watched the sauce drip down Brian's chin. Alan, however, had no problem consuming the enormous burger and reached the finish line well ahead of Brian. While he waited for his dinner companion to finish his meal, Allan absent-mindedly watched an American football match on the TV in the corner. 'What a stupid game,' he thought, 'what pompous asses! Idiots!'

'So, that happened once, but never again,' he heard Brian say. 'A loss like that is simply unacceptable. We definitely have to win the championship, especially on home ground, in front of our own crowd.' Allan had not expected anything else. He knew the eyes of all the English fans would be on his team. They were the favourite. A team with Hawkins, Cookson and a few other aces couldn't lose. '30 May,' Brian said, 'you need to make sure we win 30 May. I'm counting on you.'

In the taxi to home, Allan mulled over the conversation. It had not been a surprise. He knew there would be no mercy if his team failed. He heard his phone ring. 'Not again,' he thought. The last thing he needed was the man with the deep voice. But it was Valerie. 'Let's go out for dinner this week,' she said. 'Have some fun. You don't have enough fun in your life. Always stress, that stupid cricket. I'll make a reservation at the Palomar. Alistair told me about it, he eats there often.'

'Fine,' Allan said wondering who the hell Alistair was. 'Fine, I'd like that.' The rest of the ride home he thought about Valerie. Yesterday, she had not served him the usual burnt steak and potatoes, but had instead laid out a fancy four-course meal which she had obviously spent a lot of time and care preparing, and this morning too, she had worn an outfit that had taken his breath away. 'Maybe I should pay more attention to her,' he thought, 'maybe I've neglected her too much.' He sighed. In a few hours, the first field practice would begin. He was not looking forward to it.

9

Vinoo

VINOO STOOD ON THE top of the stairs of the private jet that had flown him from Mumbai to Dharamsala in the northern part of India. He took a few moments to take in the dazzling view of the distant mountains. Every time he came to visit his grandfather, he was overwhelmed by the magnificent vista of the high snowy peaks.

He walked across the tarmac to the arrival gate and waited outside for Khandu, his childhood friend, to pick him up. He had not seen him for a long time, this man with whom he had spent so much time in the past. Khandu did not have a cricket bone in his body, but he had always bowled for him in those improvised cricket fields of their past. That this friend, along with his wife, was willing to take care of his grandfather filled him with warmth and love.

It was hot, but it was a fresh, light heat, exactly why his grandfather had left his village near Mumbai—to enjoy his remaining years in the pure mountain air. Here, the asthma which plagued him in the lowlands was manageable. Vinoo wondered in what state he would find the old man. Khandu and his wife's last few messages had been discouraging. He knew the two caretakers he had employed did their very best to make his grandfather comfortable, but now, the end seemed inevitable.

That's why he was here. He, the star player and heart and soul of the Indian team, should have been participating in the practice matches, where he was sorely missed. A few more days and they would travel to England, cheered on by a nation that would consider anything less than the title an unacceptable disappointment.

The sound of the BMW's horn made him jolt. He had bought the car for Khandu so he could comfortably chauffeur his grandfather around on the rare occasions he was able to leave the house. Khandu was a small man with an open mouth and brilliant blue-black hair that parted naturally in the middle. He embraced Vinoo who stood surrounded by a group of wide-eyed fans. 'You're a hero!' Khandu said as he dropped Vinoo's bag on the back seat. 'Even in this remote area you can't walk down the street unnoticed.'

Vinoo smiled to himself. He would never get used to the fame of recent years. Ever since he had scored 153 beautiful runs in his debut with the Indian team in a Test against Australia his name had not disappeared from the headlines. He was hailed as the new Tendulkar, and some even speculated that his talents surpassed those of the Little Master.

Khandu seemed undaunted by the chaotic traffic. Defying death, he manoeuvred through the frenzy of dilapidated Suzukis and Tata trucks with 'Blow Horn' signs painted on their backs—a redundant sign, as everyone blew their horns constantly. 'He who breaks last laughs loudest!' exclaimed Khandu, as he overtook a car, barely making it back in the lane on time. When a skinny cow suddenly appeared on the pothole-infested road, they had an even closer call.

'How is the great and famous friend of mine?' he asked as if the near-fatal incident never happened. 'What do you think of our chances in England?' Vinoo smiled faintly. 'A question requiring a cliché answer,' he thought. 'We have a chance,' he said, 'but that goes for most teams. Everyone is armed to the teeth.' Khandu felt his friend's mood and changed the subject. 'The old man spends his days staring into space,' he said quietly. 'Since your grandma died, he has barely uttered a word. He does utter your name now and again. He will be so happy that you're here, despite your crazy life.'

Stuck in a thick traffic jam, not able to inch forward or backward, Vinoo took in his surroundings. To the right of him, he observed a large poster promoting his favourite chewing gum, Orbit. Next to the poster, a man was stencilling a Coca-Cola advert on a roller door. The three-legged dog with half a tail next to the man reminded Vinoo of his faithful companion, Six. Six had not been a beauty either, but when Vinoo hit the tennis ball with his homemade bat far out in the field near his house, he always fetched it for him, without fail. Sadly, Six was killed by a taxi driver who hadn't even bothered to stop.

Half an hour later, Vinoo spotted the gold-leafed red fence that surrounded his grandfather's mountain home. He was anxious. He couldn't help but feel this might be the last time he would meet him. The old man might die while he was in England with the team. Hesitantly, he walked into the bedroom where his grandfather was resting. The heavy drapes were closed. It took some time for his eyes to adjust to the gloom and see the dark spot on the bright white pillow. His grandfather was asleep, mouth half-open and snoring gently. Approaching his grandfather, Vinoo noticed the old man had deep brown blemishes on his face that hadn't been there before. 'Age slowly eats you,' he thought, 'but you don't give up.'

He sat down on the chair next to his grandfather's bed, took his hand and gently stroked it. This was the man to whom he owed everything. The man who'd planted the cricket seed which had now come to fruition. His grandfather suddenly heaved a deep sigh and slowly opened his eyes. Although he looked in Vinoo's direction he did not appear to see him. Vinoo looked into the empty eyes where the white had turned yellow over the years. 'It's me, Grandfather,' he whispered so as to not frighten the old man. 'Me, Vinoo, the boy you used to tell your stories to.'

His grandfather's eyes briefly lit up. 'Nayudu. C.K. Nayudu,' Vinoo heard, 'Bombay 1926.' 'And Ganish,' said Vinoo, 'your friend who fell off a tree.' But his grandfather had drifted away to distant, faraway places. Vinoo sat by his side, quietly remembering all the stories. After half an hour, Vinoo bent over and kissed the old man lightly on his forehead. 'Bye bye, Grandfather,' he said. 'Goodbye.' He knew this was the last time he would see his grandfather alive.

Deeply moved, Vinoo walked to the greenhouse in the back of the garden, where his grandfather cultivated special plants. He stopped when he came to the yellow oleander, a particular favourite of his grandfather. While crushing the seeds, his grandfather used to tell him to be very careful with them. Only in very small dosages could the plant be used as a medicine, but too much could be deadly. The heat in the greenhouse got the better of Vinoo. It wasn't much better outside but at least he wasn't suffocating.

Later that afternoon, he and Khandu got in the car and took a short trip down memory lane. His friend stopped and pointed high up in the mountains. Vinoo knew exactly what he was pointing at, it was one of the reasons he had made the trip up north. He had wanted to see this. Behind a small field he recognized the thin strip of compact dirt which left little to the imagination. On this primitive cricket pitch, surrounded by small and large boulders in the outfield, young boys were dreaming of following his footsteps. Vinoo walked to the school across the pitch but it was empty. He ventured around to the back where he saw the sign on door which read, 'Character runs faster than a man.'

Encouraged by these wise words, he returned to the car

where Khandu waited patiently; but not before he had dropped
an envelope with a substantial amount of money in the mail slot—
money intended for the schoolchildren who undoubtedly yearned
for better facilities. Now everyone could join the local cricket club
and play on a decent pitch.

Early in the evening, his friend brought him back to the
deserted airport where the only aircraft was the Falcon, provided
by his sponsor Jet Airways, which allowed him to travel free
throughout India. Boarding the plane, he reflected on his visit and
realized he was close to tears. He loved his grandfather the most.
He would miss him terribly.

Mumbai was busy and they hovered for half an hour in a holding
pattern before they could land. With the airport formalities
completed, he waited for the Mercedes which was always at his
disposal and was driven to the players' hotel. His driver Kanwar,
who clearly believed he was protected by the Jesus figurine fixed
on his dashboard and the blue plastic rosary dangling from his
rear-view mirror, sped his car at sixty miles per hour over the rough
roads. Mumbai at night was quieter than the loud, stinking mayhem
of the day, but not by much. Vinoo turned down the window to
get some air. The heat was muggy and dirty and stuck to his skin
like foil. The taxi dropped him off in front of the Taj Mahal Hotel.
He crossed the street, perilously dodging traffic, and felt the light
breeze coming in from the bay caress his face. The pressure in his
chest reminded him of miracles that were expected of him.

10

Mohammed

T HE MIRROR HAD NEVER been his best friend, although, judging by the many hours he spent in front of it, one would never guess. Sometimes he held his face just inches from the glass, as if the proximity would help explain what was wrong. He wished he looked like his childhood hero Imran Khan, the man with the movie star looks, the man whose movements on the cricket field were invariably described by journalists as 'poetry in motion'.

But Mohammed knew he was nondescript at best. That had been useful in his days as a killer, but now that his career had taken a different turn and Javed Hussain was no longer preventing him from chasing women, it would have been nice to be a bit more attractive. That was one of Javed's fundamental rules: 'No woman, they distract; stay focused.' And Javed was very strict. Mohammed made a funny face and turned away from the mirror. Leaving his hotel room, he thought about his brief conversation with James Hawkins. It hadn't been much, but it was a start.

'To the memory of cricketers of all nations these gates were erected.' Mohammed Musa paused to let the words sink in. Here he was, the

simple Pakistani boy, at Lord's—where it all began. He had bought
a ticket for a tour of the home of cricket. It was important to get
a clear picture of the turf where his men would do the work for
him during their important matches. The museum was the starting
point and about thirty interested people had gathered for the tour.
'My name is Graham,' their guide, a man with an impressive 1980s
quiff, said.

He was dressed in a blazer with an oversized club logo on
the breast pocket, skintight black trousers—leaving nothing to the
imagination—and black shoes with yellow laces and thick crepe
soles. His dry sense of humour was immediately apparent; they
would not be bored. 'He died a gallant death,' he said, pointing
to a stuffed sparrow, hit by Indian bowler Jahangir Khan in 1936.
A fat know-it-all with a grimy grey-rimmed shirt collar standing at
the front of the group immediately added that Tom Pearce was the
man about to receive Khan's ball. 'Whatever,' Muhammad thought;
this was definitely the type of person he had to stay far away from.

From the museum, they crossed to the Long Room and
through to the English team's dressing room. 'Everyone has their
permanent seat here,' Graham said. 'If a rookie, not aware of this
cardinal rule, sits on a "reserved" seat, his kit is thrown across the
room.' Mohammed looked at the green-grey carpeting—interior
design in England was clearly uncharted territory—and jumped
when someone nudged him. 'That's Michael Cookson's seat,' said
Graham, a finger pointing in Muhammad's direction, 'and once
it was Freddy Trueman's. You all know Fiery Fred, don't you?'
'The first bowler to take 300 Test wickets,' the know-it-all blurted
out.

Mohammed felt a wave of aggression rise in him. To distract
himself, he looked around the locker room. What struck him most
were the rickety physiotherapy tables, the black, cracked vinyl

benches, the merciless fluorescent light and cheap-looking gold coat hooks. Not quite what you'd call comfortable. Graham directed the group through the guest dressing room and from there, outside.

After he showed them the eight-feet slope of the field towards the Thames and shared a few more random information, it was time for the last question. 'Who hit the first and only ball over Lord's Pavilion, took two hat-tricks in the same first-class inning and played for England as well as Australia?' A dead silence ensued, even the fat know-it-all kept his mouth shut.

'Albert Trott.' Muhammad was startled by his own voice and embarrassed that he had not controlled himself. But he owed his father this. Not only had his father left him his knife, he had also bestowed upon him a substantial knowledge of cricket facts. 'Albert Trott, nicknamed Albatrott,' he heard himself say. 'Trott, who in his 1907 benefit match took so many wickets in such a short time that the match was over before one knew it.'

On the way out, he found himself walking behind the fat know-it-all who had almost ruined the tour for him. The man waddled like a duck, but kept a considerable pace. As if drawn by a magnetic force, Mohammed followed him. A few hundred yards further, the man turned left. Muhammad's hotel was in the exact opposite direction, but he continued trailing the waddler. The man stopped at a kiosk at the entrance to St John's Wood Station, bought a newspaper and went inside. Other than the two of them the platform was deserted. The know-it-all was soon engrossed in his newspaper.

Muhammad felt the hot wind of the oncoming train and sensed his hand reach for the man's back. In his mind's eye, he saw his screaming victim crashed to the rails. Restraining himself cost Mohammed superhuman effort. Rushing to the exit he knew he had *almost* made a horrific mistake. Murder in broad daylight. All of Scotland Yard would be after him. He shuddered at the thought.

11

Michael

'POKER IS A TOP-LEVEL sport. After a few hours, I'm a total wreck; wiped out.' The man beside Michael had a handsome yet weathered face, as if life had taught him a few too many lessons. 'Another whisky?' he asked. Michael nodded. His nerves were tightly strung, something he never experienced at the wicket. 'Yesterday I had four-of-a-kind and thought I had it made. Then I was hit with a royal flush.' The man sighed, 'That did it for me.'

Michael nodded sympathetically, he knew the feeling; he could have been describing Michael's recent poker nights. Even when he was dealt a fantastic hand, there was always someone who had a better one. The damp spots under his arms were proof this was another one of those nights. He didn't mind losing a few thousand pounds; what irked him and gave him heartburn was the fact that he had lost to a man with owlish glasses who probably couldn't count to ten.

After abruptly ending the conversation, he hurried to the exit. He had intended to walk, but the pouring rain forced him into a taxi. He was tired and wanted to go home. Maybe a few glasses of whisky would help him sleep. His recent insomnia perturbed him immensely. He used to look down on people who could not fall asleep the minute their heads hit the pillow. Not him; he slept like a log, always. But since the trips to Barbados and the USA, he had not had a decent night's sleep. The first few nights, he had tried a cup of warm milk and honey. When that didn't have the slightest effect, he had gone to see William Hutton, his general practitioner. Friendly, yet insistent, he had asked his GP for help; 'I don't care what you give me, as long as I get at least seven hours of sleep.'

William had looked at him closely; he had wanted to ask about the cause of his insomnia, but had chosen to remain silent. 'Let me start you on Temazepam,' he had said, 'not sure if it will help you, it's a very light sedative. But just try it, we can always switch to something stronger.' Michael had asked Carine to pick up the prescription and that evening he had taken two capsules. He had read somewhere that the effect of the drug is intensified by alcohol, so he had downed two glasses of whisky. Three hours later, he had woken up with a splitting headache and an indescribable nausea which wouldn't ease up. He had never felt that bad after a few drinks, so it had to be the pills; it had taken quite some effort to restrain himself from flushing the Temazepam down the toilet.

On his way back home from the casino, Michael wondered about Carine. She would probably not be home. These days she usually stumbled in late at night reeking of alcohol. He needed to end their relationship, soon. Carine was going downhill. He knew she was unfaithful to him, and he couldn't care less. Plenty of fish in the sea. He thought of karateka Muriel and shuddered. He had been thinking a lot about her lately. James was the only one in the team he had told about his obsession with the woman who had kicked him to almost impotency. He had smiled condescendingly. 'You'll get over it,' he had said with a straight face, 'you may not think so now, but take it from me, I speak from experience.'

An old classmate had recently told Michael that Muriel was

dating a non-athletic poet who resembled Ted Hughes, the only poet he could bear. Michael had feigned indifference, but inside, he was still enraged. He had not forgotten that kick in the balls. One day he would make her pay. The taxi slowed down. Michael pulled out a twenty-pound bill, but the driver waved it away, 'I won't take your money, Mr Cookson, just get me a century!' The driver got out of the car and opened the door for Michael. He felt embarrassed, especially when the driver tipped his imaginary hat.

Michael knew he held a preferred position in the team. As Londoners, he, Allan and Tony were afforded an extra week at home, in the luxury of their own beds. After that, they too, just like the rest of the team, would make their way to the Danubius Hotel—in his present tipsy state, this made him quite happy. A night like last night would be impossible. He was not really drunk, but he certainly was tipsy. It felt as if the all the recent stress was affecting his otherwise indestructible constitution. On the sidewalk, he paused, rummaging for his keys. It was 3 o'clock in the morning. He fumbled with the key and unlocked the door. The house felt chilly. He had come to hate the interior, so carefully designed and decorated by Carine. She may have read every interior designing magazine available, but it didn't do much to improve her taste. Michael often longed for his messy room at Cambridge. Those were the days. He fetched a bottle of whisky from the kitchen and settled back into the cushions of their oversized white leather sofa, longing for oblivion.

The slamming of the door almost gave him a heart attack. Carine was clearly not even trying to enter the house quietly anymore. With blurred vision, Michael saw a cornflower blue dress with a ravine-deep neckline. 'Pour me one,' she said, pointing to the half-empty bottle. When Michael, woozy as he was, made no move to cater to her demand, she poured herself a generous glass and flopped down beside him. 'How's my little man?' Her cajoling voice made Michael sick. 'I asked you a question,' she continued. 'I asked how you are doing. But maybe I don't need to ask. You just sit there like an old corpse.'

Despite his intoxicated state Michael's sense of honour was deeply offended. He, the Greek god Adonis, an old corpse? 'Where have you been, you slut?' he said, sitting up straight. 'You look like a third-class whore.' Carine looked at him for a while and laughed out loud. 'Well, that's more to your taste, isn't it?' she said when she had calmed down. Michael leaned over to pour a glass and suddenly felt a slap on his hand. 'You've had enough,' he heard, 'little man must go to bed now. Otherwise little man will be a drunken man.'

When he came to his senses, he couldn't remember a thing. It was evident that Carine, lying between the coffee table and sofa, had stopped moving. A red bruise circled her throat. Her dress was scrunched indecently high, exposing her bright red thong. Her stiletto heels dangled strangely from her feet. Michael's blood rushed through his veins. He had done it; now he would have to bear the consequences. He sat on the couch looking at the dead body for a while, in particular at Carine's cell phone peeking out of her bra.

He put the phone on the table and sat down again. He had slept with this woman; he had played out his wildest fantasies with her. Albeit she had endured him more than participated, it still counted for something. That his deed would have major consequences hardly registered with him. He was sitting in his house with his girlfriend's corpse; that was pretty much it. This is where the world stopped turning. He jolted out of his alcoholic haze and realized he could not sit there all night. He reached out and pulled her dress down. He picked up his phone and called Tony.

12

Tony

LATELY, PHYSIOTHERAPIST TONY ABBOTT'S dreams were vivid and troubled. The starring role in his dreams was invariably his ex-wife, Helen's. Sometimes she reproached him bitterly and then she seduced him wildly with her sweetest smiles and most enticing outfits. That's how it used to be in real life too. Tony had fallen for Helen in a big way and in the beginning she was sweet and tender. And sexy—it had seemed as if she couldn't get enough of him. But after a year, her sweetness proved mostly superficial. Her biting comments were, more often than not, too sharp. Because he never knew what to expect of her, he became increasingly insecure.

And Helen could not get pregnant. It was inevitable that she pointed to him as the guilty party and her mood became increasingly dark. Extensive medical tests revealed she was barren and he as potent as a stallion. Things went from bad to worse, so last fall's blow-up had been no surprise. 'You're boring,' she reproached, 'and you're never here. I might as well not be married. I want a divorce.' The affair with Kevin Higgins, a real estate agent—a blagger he despised—had unhinged him for quite a while. But despite everything, in his way, he had been crazy about her. Of course Allan had supported him in those dark days; that's what best friends do. Surprising was Michael Cookson's support, he had revealed a completely unknown side of himself. Most people, including Tony, regarded Michael as a highly talented, but an arrogant prick. But this was a very different Michael, a sensitive Michael. During the West Indies tour Michael had sat at his table several times, always asking how he was, always offering support.

And now, he needed him. The ringing phone abruptly woke him from his dream—Helen was in the middle of a vile tirade—and he needed a few seconds to get his bearings. 'Jump into your car immediately,' Michael said. 'Something bad has happened. I can't tell you on the phone.'

He covered the distance from his place to Michael's in record time. The old Vauxhall, replacing the expensive John Cooper Works he had surrendered to Helen, had not failed him so far, and brought him safely to his destination. Given the urgent tone of Michael's call he expected to find him waiting at the door, but that was not the case. It took at least three minutes for the front door to open.

Michael was drunk, that was obvious. Unsteady on his feet, he leaned against the wall for support. He beckoned Tony inside and led him into an office-like room to the right of the front door. Tony sat down at the desk while Michael remained standing, an unlit cigarette between his fingers. 'I thought you were vehemently against smoking,' Tony said. 'Weren't you in a TV ad warning children of the dangers of tar and nicotine?' Michael did not respond, but stared blankly at a spot behind Tony as if he would find the solution to his problem there. 'Carine is dead,' he said flatly after a while. 'I don't exactly know what happened, but I think I strangled her.'

Tony was prepared for anything—depression, health

problems, money worries, nothing would have surprised him, but this struck him dumb. 'I think you're drunk,' he said after a few seconds, 'probably hallucinating. Let me take you upstairs so you can sleep it off.' Michael suddenly appeared sober. 'Follow me,' he said, 'see for yourself.' They crossed the hall to the living room. Tony had never been in Michael's home and was awed by the grandeur and luxury. Although the light in the living room was dimmed, Tony instantly noticed that something was wrong. Carine lay motionless on the floor between the sofa and the table, her red hair fanned around her head as if aflame. Instinctively, he remembered his first-aid course and knelt beside her, but she was dead.

Strained, he stood up. Michael seemed to drift off, far away from the scene of the crime. Tony hesitated. In his heart he knew he had to call the police. A murder was a murder, even if it was committed by someone you liked. But something inside him just couldn't drop the man who had been there for him in his darkest days. And he hated Carine. No one had ever treated him with such contempt. The few times they had met she had made it quite clear that he was not in her league; not even worth a second glance. She was someone who could make someone's skin crawl. And there was something else. Without Michael Cookson, the English team was virtually powerless. If he wanted, Michael could single-handedly decide a game. They would need him soon. And not just the team's, but his own life too depended on it.

The slap on Michael's face brought him back to reality. Stunned, he gazed at Tony. 'What do you want me to do?' Tony said. 'We can't just leave her like this. It is important that we get her out of sight for now. Do you have a cellar where we can hide her?' 'Of course,' Michael said, the alcohol still heavy in his voice. 'Of course I have a cellar, a very large one.' 'Let's get her down there,' Tony said, 'not much more can be done right now, it's almost morning. Do you have a garden with a back entrance?' Michael was surprised by the question, but he nodded. 'I'll drive my car there tonight when it's dark. I have a big tent bag, she can fit easily in. The rest you'll see then.' Michael nodded. He knew that he had called the right man.

13

Dick

DICK ANTHONY ALMOST LOST his friend Phil to a busty peroxide-blonde bombshell of indeterminate age, who apparently did not know the way in the Underground—or at least pretended not to. For a woman in distress, no matter how tacky, everything and everyone had to yield. With his purple-red face and crooked legs, Phil did not look like a typical womanizer, but he definitely was one. In Allesford, he had a certain reputation. Julie, however, he had not touched. 'You deserve her,' he said after Dick told him of his conquest. 'Only the best for you.'

He pointed the disoriented blonde in the right direction and sat down next to Dick. 'Let's have a fantastic day,' he said, 'it was certainly an excellent start, don't you agree?' Dick knew Phil was referring to the hearty breakfast they had enjoyed at their hotel in Russell Square. Both were connoisseurs of a full-English breakfast, especially pork sausages and black pudding, which had indeed been excellent. After their breakfast extravagance and shopping spree, they indulged in an extensive lunch. Dick was sure he could do without food for the next 24 hours.

He looked at Phil's big belly and had the urge to lay his hand on it. 'We start with the tour,' said Phil, 'which will be great, but

I am really looking forward to watching the English team practise. I want to see how our boys are doing with my own eyes. How do you rate their chances?' 'I rate them rather high,' Dick answered, 'we really have a few cracking first-class players on the team.' 'That's a pleonasm,' said Phil—Mister Know-it-all, 'But you're right. I don't see a Cookson or Hawkins in the other teams, and let's not forget Ed Morrison. Last season he hit a double century in Leeds.' 'I know,' Dick said, 'I was there. I'll never forget the fireworks of sixes at the end of his innings. That man is fearless.'

Wellington Road radiated an atmosphere of peace and quiet. 'What a difference compared to the days when the test games are played!' said Phil, who had been there before. 'The entire street is packed then—hordes of people, coolers galore. Did I ever tell you about Scot who sat next to me a few years ago during the England India match?' Dick knew the story but shook his head; he did not want to deprive his friend of his finest hour. 'He fell asleep just after lunch. Who wouldn't—after two bottles of Chablis and half a dozen Scottish Eggs? Would have knocked me out too.'

Dick nodded and smiled, he knew what was coming. 'That afternoon, not much happened on the pitch,' Phil continued, 'so it came as a complete surprise when at the stroke of 3 o'clock a wicket fell. The crowd's reaction was lukewarm—everyone was dozing. There was barely a ripple of sound. But my Scotsman applauded loudly in his sleep. He had, as a true cricket fan should, a direct line from his subconscious to the field.' As they turned the corner into St. John's Wood Road, Dick laughed louder than was necessary.

The tour of Lord's was a hit. Graham, their guide, was an energetic young man and pulled one anecdote after the next from up his sleeve; the two-hour tour flew by. They ended up at The Nursery Ground, where the English team prepared for an afternoon of training. When Dick and Phil arrived, the players were on the field, warming up. Dick quietly tested himself to see if he could identify the players; he passed with flying colours. Allan Moorcombe was not really tough on his players. 'We certainly do things differently in Allesford,' Dick thought, enjoying the moment.

Ninety minutes later, the players called it a day and marched off the ground in single file. When Michael Cookson, lagging behind his teammates, came sauntering by, Dick used his Argus skills, gathered his nerve and approached him. There was no one around to make him look foolish in front of his idol. 'A moment for *The Northern Chronicle*?' he asked timidly as he walked to his target. 'We have a special "The World Cup" supplement and would really appreciate a few quotes.'

Of course he had expected a rejection. To get an interview, one had to apply well in advance. But what he had not expected was a punch in the nose. 'Shut up, you idiot,' he heard. 'Fuck you and your fucking little newspaper.' Though the punch involuntarily brought tears to his eyes, he saw a face distorted by anger. He felt Phil tug at his sleeve, and clutching his injured nose, he and his friend walked to the exit. 'He has not heard the last from us,' said Phil. 'Captain or not, he can't get away with this.'

Phil's attempts to persuade Dick to file charges fell on deaf ears. 'What's the point?' questioned Dick. A few hours later, he whisked Dick off to The Araki for an exclusive evening with Mitsuhiro Araki, the famous sushi chef. 'You know that this is made of cypress wood?' Phil commented as they sat on two of the nine seats at the bar, where they could closely watch the chef perform his magic. 'No,' Dick said, 'but I'm pretty sure I've heard that a small menu here costs 300 pounds.' 'Not relevant,' replied Phil. 'I'll cross that bridge when I get to it. I'm just following my shrink, Dr Simpson's, advice. The first and the last time I saw him he said: "Enjoy Mr Edmunds, enjoy, enjoy." He obviously didn't need to tell me twice.'

Phil boasted a single consultation with the famous shrink had been enough for him. 'His hourly rate was even higher than mine,' he said, indignantly thinking back to his brief therapy session.

'That was excellent,' Phil said as he looked over the bill with a grin, 'worth every penny.' He rubbed his belly, satisfied, as a polite burp escaped him. 'That's probably a spicy bill,' Dick said. He leaned over the table and gripped his friend by his wrists. The fact that his eyes were moist did not embarrass him at all.

14

Mohammed

MOHAMMED LAY DOWN ON the bed briefly to recuperate from the pursuit of that irritating ass. Things could have gone disastrously wrong; luckily, they hadn't. He awoke from an unintended sleep all but refreshed. He drank a glass of water to shake his grogginess—to no avail. His shirt was wrinkled and he considered changing, but then decided against it. He had to hurry. Graham, the guide, had told him his tour ticket also granted access to the England team's training which began precisely at 4 o'clock. That would give him an excellent opportunity to see all the players.

Outside, he nodded to Hirohito who politely nodded back three times while tipping his high hat. Luck was on his side; a few doors from the hotel, he spotted Lord's Pharmacy. A pretty black-haired Pakistani woman, with her headscarf pushed so far back he was almost tempted to nuzzle her neck, recommended a bottle of nux vomica. 'This should help,' she said, 'and it's homeopathic.' She was even kind enough to fetch him a glass of water so he could take the medicine then and there. Just the thought that he had an active drug in his body made him feel better as he walked up St. John's Wood Road. Traffic was at a standstill; a taxi had rammed into the back of a double-decker bus.

Zigzagging across the road through the loud honking cars, he bumped into Graham who was apparently done for the day. They greeted each other as old friends and Mohammed complimented his guide on the humour-peppered stories which had made the tour exceptionally enjoyable. Graham accepted the compliment with a slight bow and attempted to continue on his way, but Mohammed wasn't done. 'Do you know all the players on the English team personally?' he asked, 'Do you ever socialize with them?' Graham was flattered by the perceived 'insider knowledge' he had been attributed. He combed his impressive crest back and took on a serious stance: 'They all greet me,' he said after a few seconds, 'and sometimes we exchange a few words, but Ed Morrison is the only one I really know. He's genuinely interested in cricket history. He always listens attentively, and enjoys all the old legends.'

'And Michael Cookson?' Mohammed asked casually, 'What's he like?' Graham looked at him in surprise. 'Cookson is unapproachable,' he said. 'He is more important than God. And he has an awful girlfriend. An absolute bitch.'

'Really?' Mohammed replied, his ears pricked, 'How do you know?' 'She doesn't even deign acknowledging you in passing, she's so full of herself.' Mohammed felt slightly disappointment by the scanty information but left it at that. 'I have to go,' he said, 'the players are waiting!'

He passed the Tavern and along the Mound Stand to the Nursery Ground where the team was training. He was disappointed by the number of fans that had made the effort to come and watch their heroes practise. 'No more than 80,' he estimated. Mohammed settled himself in front of the Nursery Pavilion and soaked in the mood. Next to him, two men stood debating the qualities of the players. As far as he could tell, they knew what they were talking about.

They were a strange pair. Both about the same height, but that was all they had in common. The man farthest from him had curly blonde hair, a handsome face despite a scar on his upper lip and an athletic build; the other, with his back to Mohammed, had a bald spot on the top of his head and was distinctly bow-legged. They were obviously best friends. They amicably slapped each other's shoulders several times and Mohammed even watched them high-five each other. The atmosphere in the field was decidedly less enthusiastic. It was downright lacklustre. 'If that sluggish bunch is supposed to win the World Cup, then we're in real trouble.'

Michael Cookson looked particularly apathetic. He stood near the boundary, shoulders sagging, lethargic and cutting corners. As he turned around to reach for a bottle of mineral water, Mohammed saw his face and was shocked. He looked as if he had been out on the roads three nights in a row. His skin was sallow and sagging, and his eyes were red-rimmed as if he had rubbed them after a good cry repeatedly. No, he was definitely not in good shape. At 5.30 p.m., Coach Allan Moorcombe called it quits. The players wandered off the field, with Michael Cookson lagging behind.

Standing behind the two best friends, he watched the players leave. There was laughter, pushing and shoving; they were clearly enjoying themselves. But not Michael Cookson, he trailed behind, looking like shit.

In slow motion, Mohammed watched what happened next. The curly blonde man approached the captain and said a few words. The captain barked a response, and then proceeded to plant his right fist in the man's nose. The victim stood dumbstruck clutching his head while Cookson walked through the door of the indoor cricket school as if nothing had happened. Mohammed was tempted to see if the curly blonde was okay, but instead he turned away and walked slowly back to his hotel. He was delighted.

15

Michael

Michael could have kicked himself. Just when he needed to lay low, he had lost control. Luckily, he had been reasonably inconspicuous lately—no rumours—so this might go unnoticed. But one never knew. And then there was the guy he had punched. Michael knew only too well that he had hit him hard. The damage could be considerable. As a well-trained athlete, his physique steeled by frequent visits to the gym, he sometimes forgot his own strength. He took a shower and tried to put the incident behind him. If the journalist decided to press charges he would flat-out deny it. He, the great Michael Cookson, the man captaining the English team to a World Cup victory, could hardly be tempted to punch some insignificant hack. And besides, he had more important things on his mind. Tonight, at 11 p.m., Tony would meet him at the back entrance of the house to help him get rid of Carine's body.

As he drove through the gates of Lord's, the clock on his dashboard read a few minutes past six. Five long hours to go. After Tony and he had carefully laid Carine's body on the cold basement floor, Michael had gone to bed and slept like a baby—without temazepam. He had felt refreshed when he had woken up, and surprisingly, not hungover. In his first waking moments, he vaguely remembered something drastic had happened but couldn't quite recall what. But when fully awake, the night's events slowly came back to him. He did not panic. Not until he cracked open the basement door to verify he had not been dreaming did he break into a cold sweat and nearly passed out.

Back in the house, it took him considerable effort to force himself to fry a steak—after all, a man must eat. But the stench of the frying meat made him too nauseous to even take a bite. A drink on the other hand would go down nicely. The urge to reach for the bottle was almost irresistible. 'An alcoholic in the making,' he thought bitterly. 'In times of stress, there is always the bottle.' Three times his hand went to the eighteen-year-old Glenlivet on the coffee table and three times he managed to restrain himself. The fourth time however, he couldn't resist and poured himself two fingers. 'Perseverance,' he thought, 'the next one will be better.' And he was right. After his fifth glass he had reached such a state of oblivion that he couldn't care less about anything, including the dead Carine.

He must have fallen asleep. Tony's voice drifted into his subconscious from far away. 'It's time,' his friend and confidant said. 'Looks to me like you've tied one on, go take a cold shower. That should fix you.' 'I'll be fine,' Michael said, 'just give me a minute.' He stood up and stretched strenuously, feeling a shoulder muscle strain. 'Careful,' Tony said in response to his expression, 'we can't afford any injuries now, we need you strong and fit.'

Carine lay peacefully, her white, waxen face almost Madonna-like. They had arranged her is such a way—arms stretched alongside her body—that they were able to slip her into Tony's tent bag easily. After awkwardly lugging her up the basement stairs, her head bumping hard against the wall and her dress getting stuck to a nail, Tony grabbed Michael's arm and said, 'Initially, I thought Southend

Pier might be a good place, but on second thought, it's too risky. Too much open space, especially if we have to haul her on a dolly. We might be seen. So it's Bisham Woods. Close by, not more than twenty miles and plenty of spots where no one ever goes. I used to go there for walks with Helen.' He paused. Michael could tell by the frown on his brow that the memory haunted him. 'And I brought a shovel,' Tony continued. 'By the way, I followed your bad example and started smoking again.'

The Vauxhall was old, but it had a big boot. Rigor mortis had set in, but after the necessary pushing and shoving, Carine eventually fit in. 'With my luck, I'll end up breaking her bones,' Michael thought, shuddering at the gruesome thought. While loading Carine into the trunk he had checked the neighbouring houses for lights, thankfully, they were all pitch black. They drove to Bisham Abbey in silence. Tony smoked four cigarettes, inhaling deeply. The nausea Michael had washed away with alcohol was back, it was so bad they had to stop the car twice so he could vomit by the side of the road. By half past one they reached Bisham Abbey and a few minutes later, the first trees of the woods loomed ahead of them. Tony dimmed the car lights, reduced the speed and found a spot to park at the edge of the woods. 'If we go far enough into the woods and bury her deep enough, no one will ever find her,' Tony said. He opened the boot and gestured Michael to get to work. Tripping and stumbling from the weight of the body, they moved off the path. Luckily, there was a crescent moon in the sky, so they didn't need their flashlight—something Tony wanted to avoid at all cost.

At about a fifty yard's distance they stopped under a large beech; at least Michael thought it was a beech as he leaned against the smooth trunk to catch his breath. 'Let's not start randomly digging,' Tony said. 'We might be far from civilization but it is best we disturb the earth as little as possible.' Exploring the terrain he eventually settled on a spot a few feet from the tree. 'You do the heavy work,' he told Michael. 'you're in good condition.' Michael, for the umpteenth time, wanted to throw up. But maybe because his stomach was empty or maybe because he knew he had to gather himself, he gained control of his nausea.

The ground was fairly soft but it still took them—with Michael doing most of the digging—more than an hour to dig a grave deep enough to satisfy Tony and to ensure that no burrowing animal could disturb Carine. 'It has to be a dignified burial,' Tony said. 'We can't just dump her in that pit. Pass her to me,' he said as he jumped into the hole and held his hands up, to reach for Carine. At that moment, the shrill sound of his ringtone and favourite song—'Driver's Seat' from Sniff 'n' the Tears—shattered the silence of the woods. He froze. He had forgotten to turn his bloody phone off. He reached into his pocket and saw that Helen had chosen this unholy hour to reach out after being incommunicado for months. He quickly turned the phone off. He reached up again, took Carine's body and gently laid her at his feet. He then scrambled to get out of the hole as fast as possible. The soft walls of the grave crumbled underneath his feet and despite Michael's help it was a challenge to get out. As they closed the grave the only sound that could be heard was of earth falling on Carine's body, slowly covering her up.

On the way back, neither spoke. 'I hope you've come up with a good story,' Tony said after a while. 'You'll need one. Questions will be asked, count on it. Did Carine have parents? Brothers and sisters?' 'No,' Michael replied, 'she was an only child and her parents died in a car crash a few years ago. She did go out a lot in London, but I don't think she really had friends.' 'Good,' Tony said. 'Stick to the story, tell people she left you and you have no idea where she is. Suggest a lover and get rid of some of her clothes and make-up, make your story plausible. It shouldn't be too hard.' 'Sounds like a plan,' Michael said, 'I'll do exactly that.' 'And now I'm done talking,' said Tony, 'I never talk this much.'

16

Vinoo

VINOO DID NOT KNOW how long he had been standing listening to the whispering of the sea. It must be late. His teammates and team manager might be worried about him, but he was not ready to go in. His head was too full of thoughts and he decided the hotel could wait for another hour. He crossed the road and walked along the Gateway of India into the city—something he could never do during the day, when he needed bodyguards to protect him. Compared to those musclemen, he was very small, but then they couldn't play cricket. He chuckled to himself while walking past the darkened shop windows; it was too dark to make out what they were selling.

He felt an urge to do something reckless. He started to run. That would have made the headlines: 'India's biggest sports hero running in the streets of Mumbai and nobody to witness it.' He picked up speed, running even faster. He felt free, free of all the hassles of the team, free of the thought of his grandfather's imminent death. Free. But suddenly, something hampered his liberating run. His arms flailed as he staggered to regain his balance. He had seen it happen before, during a match—a player had stumbled over his own feet, with his arms and legs unbalanced, and then he had crashed on the grass. And that was happening now. But this was different; he had not tripped over his feet, a stick had been jabbed between his legs. It took considerable effort to regain his balance and to not fall—just to save the Indian team from losing their captain on whom they so desperately depended.

Sweating profusely, he walked back to see what had just happened, when he saw a skeleton-like hand reach out from behind a pillar. The beggar looked almost inhuman. He was so emaciated his bones jabbed through his skin, both his legs were missing and he only had one arm. In contrast to his feeble body, the look he gave Vinoo was strangely powerful. Vinoo did not know what to do. He could either kick the poor bastard for what he had done to him or he could give him some money. For a split second, he remembered that his mother always warned him never to give money to beggars: 'If you start giving them money, there'll be no end. You'll be broke before you know it'. Vinoo ignored her advice and gave the man some bills from his wallet. The beggar didn't acknowledge or thank him, but just kept staring. Vinoo turned away and started walking back to the hotel.

He only noticed it after a few minutes. The tip-tapping of footsteps was faint at first. But it became louder as it came closer; as if someone, wearing tap shoes, was trying to overtake him. He started walking faster, and then began to run. He thought he had shaken off whoever was following him, but soon the tip-tapping was even louder. 'I'm a trained athlete. I should be able to outrun this person. I can't let this happen. First, a beggar and now, a mugger. This is too much for one night.' Just as he was getting ready to make a final run for it, he felt the energy leave his body; his muscles crumpled and everything around him turned black. The last thing he remembered was collapsing against a wall.

It was freezing cold. There must be a more comfortable resting spot than a hard, stone cushion. He tried to turn to get more comfortable, but it only hurt more. This had to stop. He opened his eyes. For a moment, there was only the night in sight, but after a few seconds he saw the grey pavement on which he had laid down to rest. He couldn't breathe. It was as if he was being strangled. He needed air. He felt his throat.

Panicking, he undid the tight rope around his neck. Only then did he notice the note which had been left behind. 'Don't tell anyone', it said. 'We know where to find you'. He felt nauseous. Who had done this to him? He got up painfully and walked shakily back to the hotel. Maybe it was just his imagination, but the security guard at the gate was looking at him strangely. He could see the headlines: 'India's captain reports back drunk to his hotel far past midnight.' He couldn't care less.

His grandfather stood at the boundary as usual, his grey hair blowing in the wind. He seemed to be shouting, but Vinoo couldn't hear him. He had to concentrate. 'We need a six'. They hadn't gotten a single run in the last overs. It said 499 on the board. He looked at his grandfather. It just had to work. He did not want to disappoint the old man. The full toss almost surprised him. He turned and saw a top edge fly from the bat. 'Not again,' flashed through his head. 'That's going to be an easy one for the fielder in the deep'. His eye's followed the ball; he was already feeling miserable. Near the boundary, a fielder was getting ready to catch the ball, but his fingertips barely touched the red leather and certainly didn't stop the ball. The umpire called a six with great enthusiasm. 505 runs. He had finally beaten Brian Lara. When he looked up he saw his grandfather mouth the words: 'Not out'.

He woke up at eight, still living the dream which was soon shattered by the memory of the night before. 'Don't tell anybody,' rang in his head. 'We know where to find you'.

17

Allan

'Rupert street 34,' allan Moorcombe mumbled as he climbed into the cab behind Valerie. The thought of spending a whole evening with his lawfully wedded wife had made him anxious all day. When he got home from training earlier that day, she sent him straight upstairs to show him a new light blue shirt with double cuffs and a red linen jacket. She had lain out the new branded outfit on the bed. 'I know how you hate to shop for clothes,' she said. 'That's why I took the liberty. On a night like this you have to look good; sophisticated, yet casual.' Although it was clear she wasn't expecting a reply, Allan muttered something like, 'very nice' and 'it should suit me.' 'And I shopped for myself too,' Valerie babbled on. 'Look.' She walked to her wardrobe and pulled out a muslin dress with a wide skirt. 'I'm sure you won't mind that it cost 800 pounds,' she said. 'I've hardly spent a penny on myself these last few years. And Alistair said it was time for me to go a little wild.'

Again Alistair? Allen was beside himself. 'Who the hell is Alistair?' He asked, slightly screeching. 'Our new neighbour,' Valerie answered with a smile. 'Of course you haven't met him yet, he just moved in five weeks ago. A fantastic man.' Allan was livid now. Was his mousy, dull wife suddenly screwing the new neighbour? 'No,

I haven't met him yet,' he said. 'Is he really that interesting?' That was just the question Valerie needed to spur her on.

'Absolutely!' she squealed. 'You should see his house! He's decorated it so beautifully. You know what a dark cave Eileen and Harvey used to live in, really a cave, but now everything is light and bright, with abstract paintings on the wall that apparently cost a fortune.' 'Is this fabulous man married?' Allan asked, hoping his insecurity was not audible. 'No,' Valerie said. 'He enjoys his freedom too much. A man like that isn't likely to commit to anyone. You should see him when he goes out to Compton Street on Saturday nights.' Allan could not hide his glee. 'Ah, so your boyfriend goes to gay paradise, does he?' he said. 'I should have known.'

Although Allan suspected that the driver had detoured a few miles, he kept his mouth shut and even gave him a generous tip. Inside the restaurant, a waiter brought them to a round table. Valerie chose the cobalt blue bench against the wall, and Allan sat opposite her. The place was packed so it took a while before they could place their order. Their conversation was strained. Valerie had pretended not to hear his boorish remarks that afternoon, but Allan could tell she was disappointed. She looked pale and fidgeted with her hair. 'That dress looks ridiculous on her,' he thought. 'Sticks out like a sore thumb.' Valerie seemed uncomfortable in it; she kept looking around as if she felt people were staring at her dress.

'How's our dear boy Jimmy?' he asked to break the ice. Valerie's nervousness melted like snow in the sun. She was on familiar ground now and regained her confidence. 'Not bad, not good,' she replied. 'You know he started out well, but in the recent months he seems to be slipping. I think all that pot is turning his brain to mush.' Using the word 'pot' had made her blush. Allan almost softened. Valerie had never been at home in the big scary world. 'I'll speak to him,' he said. 'A father-and-son talk might do some good.' But as he said it, he realized he had never had a conversation with Jimmy. He was always away and left it up to Valerie to handle things. 'And Melanie?' he asked. 'She's great,' Valerie said, 'studying hard, doing exceptionally well.'

The atmosphere between them relaxed and if a man wasn't occasionally staring at him, he would have almost enjoyed himself. Or was he just imagining it? Ever since the deep voice had entered his life, he had been on edge. He had never seen this man before, he was sure of it. A prominent boxer's nose dominated the man's face and his black hair was plastered down by a healthy lick of brilliantine. His light-grey suit looked expensive but the club tie betrayed his class. Allan worked at his beef tartare, which was good but nothing special, and listened as Valerie babbled on. The familiar chatter allowed him to switch her off and concentrate on the staring man who was starting to bother him. He sat alone at a table and seemed to have little interest in his food. Occasionally, he glanced at a book, but that too did not seem to hold his interest.

'So Melanie's doing great,' said Valerie, 'but you didn't react when I told you she has a boyfriend now.' Allan was shocked. Of course he loved his daughter but somehow it had never occurred to him that she would ever be associated with anyone of the opposite sex. She was too plain, too sexless. 'Not hot enough,' he often thought, 'oh well, too bad.' 'Who is he?' he asked politely, 'Have you seen him?' 'Not really,' Valerie said, 'just a picture. He looked a bit nerdish, but maybe that suits our daughter.' Allan was just about to agree when he felt a tap on his shoulder. 'Sorry to interrupt,' said a voice he did not recognize, 'may I have your autograph?'

The man stood behind him so he could not make out who it was. 'I collect autographs of the English cricket team,' the man said. 'Only yours is missing.' He placed a team photo in front of Allan which was so unflattering, he almost laughed out loud. He scribbled a quick signature and turned to see who had made the request. But all he saw was the back of a man disappearing around the corner of the bar. 'Did you see who that was?' he asked Valerie. But she had been so busy praising the amazing Alistair that she had not paid attention. Allan looked for the man who had been staring at him. His seat was empty.

18

Tony

Howebever badly his relationship with Helen had ended, Tony could not get used to an empty house. 'Hello! I'm home!' he would call out as he would open the door, but was always met with silence. Now, after this nocturnal escapade, more than ever, he longed for companionship, someone to listen to his story, to feel basic human warmth. He sank in his favourite chair, suddenly remembering the call he had silenced while standing in the grave. He fished his mobile phone from his pocket and saw that Helen had left a voicemail. He looked at the pack of Benson & Hedges on the table and decided to light one up, something to celebrate this special moment. 'Only one,' he swore to himself, 'then I'm done.'

He called his voicemail and waited anxiously. The first few seconds sounded like the rush of a waterfall, but then he recognized a hoarse and very drunk Helen slurring her words. 'Hello sweetheart,' he heard, 'long time no see. I can ask how you're doing, but I know you won't answer. Still, you might want to know I'm in bad shape.' She burst into an endless fit of coughing. Tony took a final drag of his cigarette and was about to light another when Helen's gravelly voice resumed. 'Really bad shape,' she said. 'But I think I've mentioned that already. "Shit" is actually a better word, total shit.

You know what that bastard did?' There was a pause as if she was preparing for a grand finale. Tony settled comfortably in his chair, ready to savour any abuse directed at the man who stole his wife. 'He cheated on me,' Helen continued. 'Not once, but ten times. And every time with some young bird who could have been his daughter. And you know what?' No, Tony didn't know what. 'At home,' she slurred, 'in my own bed. You know I go to my mother's every weekend? Well, that's when he did it. The bastard.'

The voicemail ended abruptly. Tony noticed how tightly he was holding the phone, his fingers cramped. He sat motionless in his chair, an unlit cigarette dangling in his left hand. What the hell did this mean? After all this time, why had Helen decided to call?

His black dirty fingernails brought him back to the last few hours. It had all been clumsy at best. Settling Carine into the narrow grave as Michael lowered her to him had been awful. The memory sent a shiver down his spine. He walked into his tiny enclosed garden. Small as it was, he had tried to create something with plants lining the tall fence. But nothing grew. Even the toughest plant could not survive his many trips abroad. What was left was an array of yellow-brown withered stalks and leaves.

In the distance, he heard his phone ring. He slowly walked inside; he knew who was calling. 'I'm so happy you answered,' Helen said as he picked up the phone. 'I hate voicemails, it's like talking to a wall. Did you hear my message?' She was still slightly drunk, but not as much as before. 'Yes,' Tony replied. 'I heard it, although I'm not sure why you told me. It's your problem.' 'You don't understand,' she said, 'I wanted you to know that I'm done with that bastard. Did I tell you he hit me? In my face with the flat of his hand, while laughing.' Tony felt himself break out in a cold sweat of rage. Helen had treated him badly when she had ran off with that dandy Kevin Higgins, but that didn't change what he had once felt for her. 'I want to come back,' she said. 'Or do you have a new girlfriend?'

Tony felt as if someone had punched him in the stomach and knocked all the air out of him. He knew that Helen could be utterly unpredictable, but this took the cake. 'Aren't you getting a bit ahead of yourself?' He heard himself mumble, 'Don't you remember calling me a boring old fart who was never home?' There was a pause. 'Yes, I did say that,' she said flatly, 'but I didn't really mean it. Actually, you're very sweet.'

Tony began to sweat again and hated himself for it.

'Let's talk about this later, when you have more control on your emotions,' he said. 'Maybe when you sober up, you'll see things differently.' 'I don't think so,' she said. 'I've thought about this a lot, more than you know. We could get a dog. We used to have Labradors when I was growing up. I loved them. I know they're a bit too in vogue now, but what do we care?' Her use of 'we' made Tony uncomfortable and besides, he hated dogs. 'Again, I think you're going a bit too fast,' he said. 'Think about it some more, I'll call you in a week. I promise.'

He glanced at his watch, it was almost 6 a.m. After last night's events, any attempt to sleep would be futile. He climbed the stairs to his bedroom, took off his clothes and prepared to take a shower. He observed his naked body in the mirror next to his bed. 'Not bad,' he thought, 'for a man of fifty, not bad.' After a few minutes under the scorching stream, he dried off his hot glowing skin and grabbed his shaving kit. This moment was sacred to him. He recalled how his father had initiated him into the secrets of a truly good shave. First, lather up intensively—well-lathered is half the job done—then, with a whetted folding knife, first shave the chin, cheeks and upper lip, lather up again and draw the knife in the opposite direction until your cheeks are blueish red.

After his shave, Tony completed the pleasant ritual by splashing Pitralon Classic on his face, his father's favourite aftershave. He went downstairs to make breakfast. He was not very hungry, but the morning training session was to start at eleven and an empty stomach just would not do.

19

Vinoo

Vinoo was grateful for the comfort of the Jet Airways Boeing 777 Business Class flying the Indian team to London; he had a lot to think about. Not only about the noose around his neck and the note, but also the call from Khandu, who had told him that the doctor hadn't given his grandfather more than a day to live. This meant that he would not be there at the cremation, he realized sadly. His thoughts drifted to the frustrating conversation he had with Aasia. The entire cricket-loving India had been in favour of him marrying the much-admired Bollywood princess; he however was not happy anymore.

His PR team had set him up with the desirable Aasia and for a while he could not believe his luck. Initially sweet and caring, impressed by his star status—far exceeding hers—she had soon become fickle and demanding. First, it was the diamond bracelet that was not exclusive enough, and then she accused him of having an affair with another Bollywood star she despised. He did have an affair, but not with someone Aasia would ever suspect. From time to time, he secretly met Deepika, his childhood love, in Hotel Vivanta in Mumbai. Vinoo's bond with Deepika was sacred, much more than the relationship with his wife.

His encounter with Dattu Lal in the lobby of the Taj Mahal hotel had left him stunned. He had known Dattu for years. He was one of the journalists who had followed him from the very beginning of his career and no one could write about Vinoo's heroic cricket exploits like Dattu. Vinoo often gave him quick interviews which were usually heralded as 'the scoop of the day'. Dattu was an impressive figure. His stomach was enormous and his shirts much too tight; a strip of his hairy belly perpetually peeped above his waistband. And he had a beard. Not just any beard but a massive beard flowing down his chest. They were on friendly terms so it had not surprised him when Dattu had pulled him aside in the hotel lobby just before leaving for England.

'I'm on the same flight,' he had said. 'And I'm staying at the same hotel in London. Maybe we could meet occasionally for some off the record information. Of course I'd pay you, you understand.' That last remark had left him in shock. Firstly, he hardly needed the money and secondly, their relationship had always been based on trust. 'I think you're talking to the wrong person,' he replied curtly. 'I'm afraid I have nothing more to say to you.' Dattu had not blink an eye. 'It can be very dangerous at night, out all alone on the streets,' had been his only comment. 'Very dangerous'.

On the screen in front of him, he noticed they were flying over the Black Sea. He attempted to focus on the Victor Trumper biography lying untouched on his lap. It was apparently an interesting read. Knowing that his illustrious hero had died much too young, he skipped to the end of the book to find the part that suited his mood—the description of the tens of thousands who took to the streets of Sydney to pay their respects in 1915. He felt tears trickle down his cheeks.

The news was anticipated, but still came as a shock. They had just checked into the London Hilton when his phone rang. He knew what was coming when he heard Khandu's voice. 'He was very restless last night,' said his friend, 'as if desperately clinging on to life. He mumbled incessantly for a while, but nothing I could make sense of.' 'And then?' asked Vinoo, 'I hope he went peacefully.' 'He did,' Khandu said, 'I sat with him till the end. By ten o'clock, he was calm. He took a few breaths and was gone. I closed his eyes for you.'

'Please take care of him,' Vinoo said, 'you know I would have liked to do it myself, but I know I can depend on you and trust you to arrange a dignified funeral.' Khandu reassured him; he hung up and sat on the bed. His mother was still alive, albeit a medical miracle, but her influence on him was nothing compared to the big grey man with the ferocious eyebrows. However high he soared in life, Vinoo never stopped yearning for his grandfather's approval.

His days would never be complete without speaking to his grandfather after an important match. Sparse with praise and never hesitant to point out his flaws no matter how perfect the inning, he would always end the conversation with 'Farewell, my boy! May my blessing be with you and keep you safe.' The solemnity of the words had always moved him.

The sound of his phone brought him back to the present, but he ignored the insistent ringing, there was no one he wanted to talk to now. He lay on the bed, clasped his hands behind his head and tried to sleep. After a few minutes, he felt a great weariness come over him. At first, he thought someone was hitting him over the head with a hammer, but it turned out to be a frantic banging on the door. 'Vinoo, Vinoo,' he heard, 'what's wrong with you? Please answer!' 'I'm coming, I'm coming,' he called. He rubbed away the sleep from his eyes, accidently spilling a glass of water on the nightstand. Of course it was Vijay who had brought him back into the land of the living.

Vijay was, after all, his friend. It was fitting that his best friend was the least talented player on the team, always dangling behind, rarely getting beyond twelfth man. He knew that without the good word he put in for him, his friend probably would not have been chosen for the trip to England, but that was perfectly all right with him. He opened the door and looked at the distressed face with the big bulging eyes. 'I thought you were dead,' his friend said, 'you sometimes hear about young people suddenly dying in their sleep.'

Vinoo smiled at his friend's concern. He put his arm around Vijay's shoulder and together they walked to the lift. The two women in the lift had doused themselves in so much perfume that Vinoo was relieved when they reached the ground floor. 'My grandfather is dead,' he said as they walked to the team meeting. 'He was old, but still.' Vijay looked at him with empathy. He knew all about the special bond between Vinoo and his grandfather.

'You'd probably want to fly home now,' he said, 'but you can honour him by getting high scores here.' Vinoo nodded. High scores were the last thing on his mind. He heedlessly bound down the three steps in the hall and felt a sharp pain in his thigh. 'Not now,' flashed through his mind, 'not before the big match.' He'd had a hamstring injury once; it had kept him on the bench for months. His worst nightmare. He felt the pain subside and then disappear altogether. Smiling, he thought of his grandfather's home remedy. He'd sworn by yellow oleander, but was always careful of its dangers.

With a sigh of relief he sat down to listen to Coach Dilawar Jilani. The Coach could be so long-winded most players sat through his sessions in a semi-comatose state. When he got up after an hour he felt the sharp pain again, but it faded just as quickly. 'Nothing to worry about,' he thought. 'Plenty of time to become a hypochondriac.' In the dining room, he sat next to Vijay. They were blood brothers, and they always would be.

20

Mohammed

RECENTLY, MOHAMMED HAD WOKEN up every morning with his eyes glued shut. The first few times it happened he panicked—had he gone blind overnight? But he was used to it now and slowly pried his eyes open. He skimmed through the newspapers looking for reports about the incident with Michael but found none. He wrote the word 'photograph' in the notebook he always had. When the time was right, he would tell Cookson he had a picture of the incident. Always nice to have an ace up your sleeve.

The traffic racing up the M25 out of London was crazy. Mohammed gripped the steering wheel of his rented Peugeot so tightly his knuckles turned white. What surprised him even more, however, was the fact that he was here. Twenty-four hours ago he had thought he would be working exclusively around Lord's, but Javed Hussain's call had made it very clear: 'You have to go to Taunton,' he said. 'Pakistan is playing a practice match against Somerset. I want you there to remind Aslam Ali of his obligations. Get on the road as fast as you can, I'll call you tomorrow.'

'Sure boss,' he mumbled subserviently. He wasn't too thrilled with this turn of events. He felt at home in London and where the hell was Taunton anyway? Some godforsaken hole in the middle of nowhere. Fortunately, his car came with GPS so he knew he had 165 miles to drive and if all went well, he'd be there in 2 hours and 52 minutes.

As he was nearing Swindon he felt a sharp pain in his back. He stopped at a roadside restaurant where he was met with an assortment of greasy foods. He chose the least dicey-looking snack on the menu—a cheese sandwich—and sat at a dirty Formica table covered in coffee stains. Just like with every job he did for Javed, he could not afford even the slightest mistake—precise preparation was vital. 'Aslam's in trouble,' Javed had said, 'and he's unpredictable. This is his first job and I don't want him to chicken out at the last moment. Pressurize him, but not enough to make him panic.' Mohammed pondered over the conversation he had with his boss. 'This should be a breeze,' he thought. 'What could go wrong?'

The gate to the Somerset County Cricket Ground was open. Nothing indicated that a big crowd would fill the seats the next day. He sat a few feet away from the only other visitor and observed the two prominent church towers in the distance. He took a few moments to absorb his surroundings, picked up his phone and tapped the number Javed had given him. 'Aslam Ali,' answered a voice softly, 'who is this?' 'It doesn't matter,' Mohammed said, hoping he sounded menacing enough. 'The only important thing is that you follow the instructions. I'll call you tonight at nine. That's all. You know what's good for you. Oh, and by the way, just to make sure, I'll be there personally. See you tomorrow.'

He hung up, pleased with his performance. The other visitor, who had been at a safe distance from him, moved in his direction, perhaps to chat, so Mohammed stood up hastily and returned to the parking lot. Still getting used to the rental car, he almost rammed it against the Red Dragon Somerset gate. 'On to the Castle Hotel,' he said to himself. Javed had said a four-star hotel would be fine;

he didn't need to be told twice.

What struck him first when he reached the hotel was the explosion of wisteria pouring down the façade of the building like a miniature Niagara Falls. He had never seen such beautiful flowers and gazed at them in amazement. He was so amazed he nearly missed the Aston Martin DB9 parked right next to him. Worth at least one or two hundred grand, he figured, although it couldn't be guessed looking at the driver. He was modestly dressed in grey trousers, light blue shirt and a dark blazer.

As they walked in the hotel, he greeted Mohammed with a voice that seemed to come from the depths of the earth. Mohammed followed him to the reception. The clock above the desk told him it was five o'clock. 'Khalid Ahmed?' The clerk asked as he pulled up his eyebrows. 'I assume you can read,' Mohammed retorted, slightly irritated and a bit worried. Surely they couldn't spot a fake ID in this one-horse town? But the clerk nodded, immediately put in his place. With the check-in completed, he walked on the soft red carpet to the spiral staircase leading up to his room. The decor was slightly more tasteful than the Danubius, but only slightly.

He dropped off his suitcase and went back downstairs. In the lounge, he sat at a table facing the only other guest, a blue-haired lady who reminded him of Mrs. Slocombe from *Are you being served*? Mrs. Slocombe picked up a magazine from the table between them, exposing a book with a beautiful image of a cricket ground on the cover. He picked up the book—*Sunshine, Sixes and Cider: The History of Somerset Cricket*. His father would have enjoyed this. Before he knew it, he had disappeared into world of the 'king of sixes,' Arthur Wellard; the tormented genius, Harold Gimblett; and Brian Langford, who served his county for as many as 21 years. The departure of the blue-haired lady tore him away from his reading.

She wrapped herself in a dark brown fur coat and crossed the lobby to the stairs. Mohammed watched as she was almost knocked over by the Aston Martin driver, sprinting like Usain Bolt to the exit. 'He's in a hurry,' Mohammed thought, 'wants to break the finish line.' The sickeningly pungent lilies in the vase next to him urged him to leave and find a place for dinner. He checked a few flyers in the lobby and chose the Blue Mango Indian. The raving text promised him an excellent experience. A few hours later, he walked through the deserted streets back to his hotel and reminded himself never to trust those flyers again. The food had been okay, but outrageously overpriced. Even though he'd be reimbursed, he still felt cheated.

21

Michael

As a precaution, michael used the back entrance to his house. He drank a glass of iced water in the kitchen, and then, somewhat hesitantly walked into the living room. Although he was determined not to invite anyone into his home anytime soon, he wanted to thoroughly check the area between the sofa and the coffee table— just in case. From the many detective novels he had read in his father's well-stocked library, he knew that even the minutest detail, the slightest clue, could lead to a horrific conclusion. He crouched on his knees and scanned the floor, but there was nothing; no blood, no hair, nothing. Only when he got up did he notice a dark stain on the edge of the table. He examined the spot carefully with his finger and was pretty sure it was blood. Not much, but blood. 'Thank God that hideous table is glass,' he thought. 'Wood would have been a problem.'

He trotted to the kitchen, tore a few sheets of paper towel off the role and grabbed a bottle of all-purpose cleaner. Armed, he went back to the living room. He scrubbed the spot clean multiple times, until he was sure that even the most advanced equipment wouldn't find any evidence. He flushed the soaked paper towel down the toilet and kept the all-purpose cleaner back into the kitchen cabinet.

Collapsing on the sofa, his situation slowly began to sink in. He was a murderer, a cold-blooded killer. If found out, he was sure some savvy lawyer could plea him down to manslaughter, but he'd definitely spend a year or ten living at the government's expense. Yet, somehow he knew in his heart it wouldn't come to that. The story Tony had suggested was simple and by virtue of its simplicity, it was brilliant.

Complex fabrications would only be suspicious. What surprised him most about his situation was his total lack of remorse. By all accounts, he should have been consumed with guilt and tearfully confessing his crime to an understanding policeman, but all he felt was self-pity. That bitch had provoked him. If she had just taken her drunken self to bed none of this would have happened. He looked at the near-empty bottle of whisky on the table and could barely restrain himself.

He could not remember falling asleep, but he had; the sponsor's Rolex on his wrist read 9:30 a.m. The awkward position in which he had slept left a sharp pain between his shoulder blades. A few stretching exercises Allan always made the players do gave some relief, but he still felt like a wreck. Collapsing back on the sofa, he realized with a jolt that he was expected at the training session in ninety minutes; the very last thing he wanted to do. He called Allan. 'I'm not amused,' Allan said, 'but not much you can do about an acute intestinal infection. I'll call tomorrow to check up on you.' Michael did not feel any better after the call—the day loomed ahead of him. How was he going to get through it?

Usually, to kill time, he would reach for a Cyril Hare. He had inherited his passion for the author from his father, who was addicted to him. The big advantage of Hare was that he had written so little you could binge-read his entire oeuvre in no time. And you could reread his books over and over again, they were that good. Michael loved the protagonists; the failed lawyer Francis Pettigrew and Inspector Mallett with his insatiable appetite, who together solved complicated crimes by creating even more complex theories. To escape his present state of mind, he picked up his favourite Hare: *Tragedy at Law*.

But Hare couldn't help him this time, reading proved too ambitious. He felt suffocated; he had to get out before he went stir-crazy. London was out of the question, he didn't want to be recognized, but escaping the city unnoticed by car was doable. He left his conspicuous Jaguar at home and took Carine's Hyundai i20 which was parked in a side street. There were no houses on that block so he could leave unobserved. He had bought the car for her in a generous mood and he was happy that he had.

But where would he go? There was only one person he could think of, one person with whom he could relax, and that was his twin brother Julian. Julian, who had no use for cricket whatsoever. In fact, he hated the sport in which his brother excelled. 'A boring game for boring old farts,' was his standard remark. He probably didn't even know the World Cup tournament was about to begin. It had been a long time since Michael had visited Ely where Julian lived on a farm with his wife Ginny and daughter Alice. The farm had been a dilapidated old hovel, but Julian had transformed it into a paradise. What Julian could do with his hands was amazing and Michael was envious of his talent.

At Saffron Walden he left the M11 and drove towards Cambridge; as if some mysterious force had taken over the wheel of the car and was bringing him back to the city of his first sporting success—and the city of his bitter experience with Muriel. The thought of his former crush made him shudder. Should he call her? The chance that she would hang up on him was big, but, 'nothing ventured, nothing gained' as his grandfather, the stunt pilot, always said. So why not? Maybe she regretted her karate chop, maybe she was trying to hide her secret passion for him. With a sick feeling in his stomach and a vague pain in the balls, he found himself in Sidgwick Avenue near Newnham.

He pulled his car up to the side of the road and called her. 'Muriel Clark,' she answered almost immediately. Michael wanted to say something, but could not produce a sound. 'Muriel Clark,' she repeated, somewhat agitated. Michael regained control of his voice and was about to answer when he heard her curse and the line went dead. 'Goddammit,' he said softly. 'Goddammit.' He had screwed it up. Tyres screeching, he accelerated to seventy and was off.

He saw the woman sixty yards ahead of him at the crosswalk with one hand pushing a pram and the other holding an obstinate child trying to escape her grip. When the child broke free, he was too late. The Hyundai swerved and he heard a sharp bang. In his rear-view mirror he saw he had done something terrible. 'Don't stop,' flashed through his mind. 'I can't have this now.' He increased the speed, tore around the corner of Grange Road and sped towards Ely.

22

Dick

DICK COULD READ JULIE like a book. The slight frown on her brow and the barely detectable quiver of her upper lip was enough for him to know something was up. But Julie let nothing on. She hugged him enthusiastically on his return from London as he lifted little Owen into his arms. For dinner, she cooked Bangers and Mash. Julie, who saw herself as a bit of a culinary chef, looked down her nose at his favourite dish, but knew he loved it and made it for him on special occasions.

After he complimented her on the meal and they put the children to bed, he could no longer restrain himself. 'OK, what's up? I know something's wrong.' 'Nothing's up,' she answered sharply, 'really, nothing.' Dick knew persisting could lead to one of their rare quarrels, but he did not ease off. 'Come on,' he said. 'I won't bite.' He put his arm around her. 'Maybe it's nothing,' said Julie, softened by his gesture. 'I just discovered it this morning and it is still very small.' Dick suddenly had trouble breathing. 'For God's sake, what is very small?' he said, louder than intended.

Julie opened her blouse and put his hand on her left breast. 'Feel this,' she said. 'I've felt it myself at least fifty times today, something's not right.' She led his hand to a spot on the lower edge of her breast, just above her abdomen, and he knew immediately what she meant. It was no bigger than a grain of corn, but it was definitely there. He kissed her gently on her nipple and pressed her close to him. 'Doctor tomorrow,' he ordered, 'waiting won't make it go away.' He felt her slide closer to him, as if she wanted to disappear within his protection. He quietly tried to extinguish the burning fear he felt.

The newspaper building where he worked was half a mile from his house. Dick loved the large, dark Victorian castle. He always walked to work, leaving Julie the Fiesta. If he needed a car, he used one of the newspaper's old jalopies. Today, he was oblivious to the small-town bustle around him which he usually enjoyed so much. To make things worse, it was drizzling. A dismal, thick, grey layer of clouds covered Allesford; not much chance of sun today. Dick pulled his raincoat tightly around him and hurried on. The article that he had to finish did not interest him in the least, but it had to be done.

He himself might have forgotten that it was his big day today, but his colleagues had not. 'Are you going to court yourself?' Leonard Black asked curiously. 'I think I might go,' Dick replied, 'I'd almost forgotten about that business with the corrupt contractor, it was months ago.'

'I'll go with you,' Leonard continued. 'Not every day that a hotshot from Allesford has to answer for his actions. I want to see him go down.'

Dick liked Leonard. Leonard was the paper's odd-job man, tasked with reporting on all kinds of events from beauty contests to Allesford United football matches—a team perpetually doomed to lag at the bottom of the fourth division. His language was baroque, his dressing style remarkable, to say the least. Winter or summer, rain or shine, even in scorching heat, Leonard was always dressed in dapper, green-brown heavy woollen suits, white shirts and multicoloured bowties. When he finally became aware of the persistent rumour that he was gay, he smiled broadly. 'Better a dashing gay than a boring straight,' he simply stated.

By eleven o'clock Dick was in all states. The article on the local protesters demonstrating against the construction of a chemical plant just inside the city limits was getting nowhere; he couldn't come up with a single word. Why the hell hadn't Julie called? She knew how frantic he was.

Desperately, he consulted his notes of the interview with one of the protesters who had spoken only in monosyllables. She had eyed him suspiciously the entire duration of the interview as if he was the personification of the anti-feminist. 'Can't make any sense of this rubbish,' he thought. 'What a stupid cow! Why do I actually even care?' A few desks down, Leonard beckoned to him. 'Bugger this, the chemical plant can go to bloody hell,' he thought and nodded affirmatively to Leonard.

The public gallery was packed. Dick and Leonard found seats in the corner with a good view of the courtroom. The defendant, contractor Craig Griffin, sat arrogantly, observing his surroundings, clearly not worried. The fact that the city official with whom he had recently done business had been sentenced to a two-year prison term did not seem to affect him in the least. Dick was hoping for a fiery courtroom spectacle, but the tedious, seemingly endless legalese made him long for fresh air.

After an hour, he tugged at Leonard's jacket sleeve and quietly suggested they go to lunch. He didn't need to convince Leonard, he was game and smiled gratefully at Dick as they left the courthouse. They climbed the stairs to the first floor of Duncan's Tearoom— obviously not a wheelchair-friendly establishment—and sat by the window. The cheery clamour in the tearoom almost made him miss the phone call. 'They did a mammogram,' Julie said flatly, 'based on the result they're doing a biopsy this afternoon. So we have to wait. But if it is malignant, then it's in its early stages. I've called the sitter and she'll stay all day.'

After the connection was broken, Dick felt somewhat relieved. 'Early stages' sounded promising. Maybe it wasn't so bad; a storm in a teacup. He ordered his favourite cheese and pickles sandwich and a glass of dry white wine. He heard Leonard order the same, with one exception; Leonard, of course, ordered two glasses of wine.

Back in the newsroom writing went a lot smoother and his piece was done by three o'clock. He looked at his watch and jolted. This was inexcusable, unbelievably stupid, how could he have forgotten? He had promised his parents he would never forget. He checked his watch again, but it was undeniably 22 May, Joe's birthday. Overcome with a deep sense of shame, he jumped up, left the building and hurried to the florist on Market Place. An unexpected ray of sunshine peeped through the clouds making the day friendlier. The florist created a beautiful bouquet costing him a small fortune, but he didn't care; after all, he had something to atone for.

The cemetery looked peaceful in the afternoon light. Dick followed the paved path through two spectacularly carved pillars leading to the plots. Joe was resting under a tree—their father had insisted on that, at least he'd have some protection there. Dick searched for his brother's grave; he hadn't visited him in a while. When he found it, he was shocked by the unkempt and sullied state it was in. It took him half an hour to scrape away the moss, firmly clinging to the grey headstone, with his bare fingernails.

When he was satisfied, he solemnly stood at the graveside and tried to remember the moment he had loved his brother the most. It didn't take long. He remembered that hot summer day when they were in a park near their parent's house playing cricket with the plastic cricket set Dick had received for his birthday. Dick was the batsman, Joe, the bowler. Joe bowled gently to his brother which the tot promptly hit for six. Dick could not have been more proud, a pride he felt to this day. Promising himself that he would visit Joe more regularly from now on, Dick left the cemetery to pick up a few things in the newsroom.

On his way to his office, he ran into Rupert Thorpe, his editor, a man as tall as he was wide. 'Have you heard?' he asked Dick as he grabbed his arm, 'Three years and not a day less. That bastard got what he deserved. And I think you deserve a reward! We're sending you as a special reporter to the World Cup. Not for the daily match reporting—Leonard can do that—but for the special-interest background pieces, columns and editorials.'

Dick was flabbergasted. 'Thank you,' he finally managed to blurt out, 'that's fantastic!' Seconds after Rupert was gone he was still catching his breath. This was great. Too good to be true. 'Thank you, Joe,' he said softly, 'thank you, big brother!'

The young rebels Ben, Harry and Owen behaved exceptionally well that evening; as if they knew something was awry. Even Harry, who usually escaped his bed at least once a night for an extra kiss and cuddle, was quiet. Dick and Julie sat next to each other on the sofa, discussing the day. 'They'll let us know the results of the biopsy as soon as possible,' she said, 'they understand how nerve-wracking this is. But they did seem reasonably optimistic.' Dick recalled the term 'early stages' and experienced the same relief as before. And he was encouraged by Julie's reaction to his new cricket assignment. 'Of course you have to go!' she said enthusiastically. 'You can't pass up such an amazing opportunity! I'll be fine.' 'Okay, but only if you are alright,' he replied, 'only then.'

Not until they were about to go to bed did he see his antique book dealer's parcel on the hall table. Despite the anxieties of the day, he could not suppress the gleeful excitement he always felt when he was about to unwrap a new treasure. Carefully, he opened the package and could not stifle a cry of joy when he saw the content. His antiquarian had finally found the book he had endlessly been searching for: *The Public School Matches and Those We Meet There* by A. Wykehamist. A genuine first edition from 1853. He gazed at the funny little drawings on the cover and felt at peace with the world.

In the bathroom, he checked cricinfo.com. The results of the friendly matches being played around the country by the World Cup participants were not much cause for excitement. But a few strange things did catch his eye. The ridiculously slow pace the Pakistanis kept against Somerset between 100 and 150, after they had bowled the first 100 in exactly ten overs, had puzzled the commentators. And that was not the only odd thing they had reported.

Closing the bedroom door behind him, he heard Julie's regular breathing; she was fast asleep. He stroked her back gently, so as not to awake her. She shivered slightly at his touch, made a soft sound, and slept quietly on.

23

Vinoo

SITTING IN HIS ROOM, Vinoo pondered over the stack of unopened envelopes. His grandfather's death had kept him too preoccupied to be bothered with mail. From the moment he became famous he had been bombarded with requests for opening festivals, shopping malls and cricket tournaments. He was even in high demand on the lecture circuit these days, both at home and abroad. Occasionally he accepted, but more often than not, he just ignored the requests; it was not his forte. He worked through the pile rapidly, tossing most aside until he came to the last letter.

The author was trying too hard, flattering him with lavish compliments, it literally made him sick: If he, the great Vinoo Ramji, would deign to spend half an hour of his undoubtedly very valuable time to enlighten the members of the Bombay Gymkhana with his insights into the noble sport of cricket, to please determine his own fee and rest assured it may be generous. Vinoo remembered the bloated bullfrog who had brutally chased him out of exclusive Bombay Gymkhana years ago and decided not to respond. The opportunity to talk down to these arrogant jerks was tempting, but even more insulting to them would be to simply not answer. Smiling, he tore the letter in half and threw it in the bin.

Apart from the mail, there was something else that demanded his attention. His PR team thought it was a good idea for his wife Aasia and him to do a commercial for a new mobile phone. The advertisement showed them having a misunderstanding which of course the attributes of the amazing new mobile phone resolved, ending with a sickly sweet reconciliation. Vinoo couldn't make up his mind. They could make a substantial amount of money, but that was hardly a motivator. He couldn't help but feel that if he said 'yes', he would be betraying Deepika—his true love—and that was much more important. For the umpteenth time he pushed the decision to the back of his mind and turned on the TV.

The images on the television set were blurry, and therefore, all the more unnerving. Men in camouflage suits were running through the screen, gripping their weapons. 'They came from the sea,' CNN reported, 'and took Mumbai by surprise. The Taj Mahal Hotel is a war zone with numerous casualties.' Vinoo froze. He had just been there, only a few days ago. He had walked through the lobby. He had eaten in the dining room. 'The terrorists are probably from Pakistan,' he heard. 'Just like in 2008. You would expect that something like this could never happen again. The Indian authorities will have a lot to answer to.' Vinoo thought of the many times he had crossed the road in front of the Taj Mahal Hotel to enjoy the balmy sea breeze. He would have walked straight into the arms of terror.

From the TV screen, the terrifying sound of artillery fire entered Vinoo's hotel room. 'It is clear that India won't let this attack last three days as it did almost ten years ago. They seem to want to end it soon, at all cost.' The CNN reporter, a short, fat man with thinning hair, seemed to be enjoying himself. He pressed his microphone close to his lips and panted heavily. 'The final attack seems imminent,' he heaved, 'we think it will all be over within the hour.' There was a cracking of gunshots, as if a violent storm was breaking over Mumbai, followed by two heavy explosions.

'The terrorists will stop at nothing,' the reporter stated. 'They have made it known that this is just the beginning.' Vinoo was suddenly exhausted. He switched off the TV, stood at the window and thought of the upcoming championship. 'This is just the beginning,' he thought, 'who knows what awaits us.' He stared at the phone, clutched in his hand and thought about calling Deepika. He would wake her if he did, but knew she wouldn't mind. He lay on the bed and imagined her beside him, hugging the pillow as if it was their child. When he and Aasia talked about children their conversation was always strained. 'Children are not good for my career,' she'd say, 'and besides, I have to watch my figure.'

As he was nodding off to sleep, his phone rang. It was an upset Vijay. 'Have you heard?' he squawked. 'Sixty-nine dead and probably more! All foreigners, shot dead, one-by-one!' In addition to the shock, Vinoo could discern a hint of sensationalism in Vijay's voice which almost made him laugh. After all, Vijay was only human. 'You seem to be enjoying this,' Vinoo commented, 'the more dead the merrier.' It was silent on the other end.

'I'm sorry,' Vijay eventually answered, 'I got carried away. Of course, it's all very gruesome. I'll leave you alone.' 'It's alright,' Vinoo said, 'I forgive you.' After the connection was broken, sleep eluded him. Tomorrow, he had an appointment with Dattu Lal. Why, in spite of their recent encounter, he had agreed to meet with that ape he really couldn't say. 'For old times' sake,' Dattu Lal had begged, 'I only need ten minutes.'

24

Mohammed

THE SCOREBOARD TO THE right of the first church tower in Taunton's Somerset County Ground showed only zeros, but that was likely to change soon. The Pakistani opener, Mahmood Ghazali, was not known to waste time and the Somerset opening bowler, Richard Barnes, was about to find that out. In his first over, he was hit for three sixes. Upset, he glanced in the direction of Mohammed Musa sitting near the boundary and braced himself for a tough afternoon.

Mohammed had slept well and felt relaxed. After the previous evening's telephone conversation and the detailed instructions the following morning, Aslam Ali appeared to be intimidated enough to follow orders. Three 'No Balls' in an over. It might seem odd, but it was completely believable. While he mulled over the situation, the Pakistanis made mincemeat of Somerset. In their 50 overs, they made 420 runs—an enormous total. During the break, Mohammed got up to stretch his legs. He walked behind the grandstand and let himself be seduced into buying a plastic cup of local cider— considered a regional delicacy. This particular cider was piss-sour, after a few sips he tossed the remains against a wall which, by the looks he received, was definitely 'not done'.

In the run-up to Aslam's second over, Mohammed felt somewhat apprehensive. He carefully followed the run and breathed a small sigh of relief when the Pakistani bowler clearly planted his foot over the line. That was one. Aslam's next ball, a yorker, uprooted the stumps and was not part of the plan, but it didn't really matter. The third and fifth ball did matter—those were the vital ones. Mohammed watched Aslam circle his arms as if preparing for the next lethal bowl and closely followed his run-up.

And yes! Again his foot was clearly over the line. Mohammed looked at the umpire expecting him to signal a 'No Ball', but nothing happened. He swore under his breath. That screwed up the whole plan. But, as if waking up from hibernation, the umpire abruptly called the foul with an excessive gesture. In the fifth ball of the over too, Aslam kept his end of the agreement. 'Mission accomplished,' Mohammed thought. 'Hussain will be pleased.'

On his way out he noticed a familiar figure in paint-stained overalls sitting on a stool, leisurely painting the fence around the grounds. He was sure he knew that man. Wasn't his face on one of the cricket cards he used to fanatically collect as a child? As discreetly as possible, he approached the painter and confirmed his suspicion. It was Andrew Caddick, the giant of Somerset and England, 6.5 feet tall and famous for taking innumerable wickets in a long career. Mohammed was tempted to ask him for his autograph, but held himself back. Anonymity was of the utmost importance. He walked back to the Castle Hotel where he saw Mrs. Slocombe in the lobby. She nodded to him kindly as if he was an old friend. He greeted her politely and then climbed the stairs, two at a time. In his room, he called Hussain. 'All good,' was all he said, as if there was never any doubt. 'Good, so we can count on that boy. Tell him to expect a bonus.'

On the way to his car, he saw the Aston Martin still parked in the same spot. The owner was nowhere in sight so he walked up to the beautiful, streamlined car and leaned over to look at the interior through the window. He saw a lot of leather and an expensive audio system. 'A beauty, isn't she?' said a deep voice behind him. He hid his shock and slowly turned to see his compatriot now dressed in a burgundy blazer. 'She does almost 200 miles an hour,' the baritone continued, 'and from 0 to 60 in four seconds. By the way, what did you think of the match this afternoon? I saw you sitting a few rows in front of me.' 'Quite boring really,' said Mohammed who had regained his composure. 'Pakistan was much too strong for Somerset.' 'Indeed,' the man said, giving Mohammed a penetrating look. 'Still, a pity about the "No Balls."'

Mohammed felt numb. 'Every match has some,' he replied, 'nothing remarkable really.' 'But three in one over?' said the man, 'On the first, third and fifth ball. It was almost mathematical.' Mohammed felt a strong urge to run away, but he restrained himself. 'Cricket's a fickle game,' he said, realizing the cliché was a sure-shot conversation killer. 'But I have to go. I have a long drive ahead of me.' 'Yes, London is indeed a long drive,' the man said, 'have a good trip.'

During the drive back to London, Mohammed felt uneasy. A few times he caught himself speeding, big mistake for someone who needed to be as inconspicuous as possible. He tried to clear his head and pushed a CD into the player—'The Sultans Of Swing' music from his youth; it usually calmed him down. When he drove into London at nine o'clock, he was his old self again. Everything would go according to plan, he was sure of it.

25

Michael

IT WAS NO LONGER safe to continue driving. The uncontrollable spasm in his leg involuntarily pumped the gas pedal at irregular intervals; Michael was a mess. He stopped at a petrol station halfway between Cambridge and Ely. If he had thought that he, a man of steel, would be unscathed by the events of last night and the crash of an hour ago, he was now sorely disappointed. His heart pumped wildly and his breathing sounded as irregular as his father's badly tuned Norton. He could not show up at Julian's in this state, they would instantly sense that something was wrong.

He bought a bottle of Coke and black coffee and paid the cashier who clearly had some problem with her larynx. She rattled a noise that Michael could not make sense of. The woman looked at him as if he was familiar to her. Her eyes drilled through his back as he walked out the door, he felt uneasy. God forbid she recognized him; that was the last thing he needed. With any luck she wasn't a cricket fan. He sat in the grass next to his car and tried to regulate his breathing with the exercises Tony had taught him—taught all the English players.

They helped; a few minutes later, he had calmed down. He threw the Coke bottle and coffee cup in a bin and prepared himself for the rest of the trip. But first, he needed to check the front of the Hyundai. A quick look was enough. The blow had been so forceful that the front bumper had come loose and was dangerously hanging to one side. He found a piece of rope in the glove compartment and made a makeshift repair. As he drove away, his mind was made up. He would get rid of the Hyundai that night.

He parked his car behind a dense growth of bushes a distance from his brother's farm. He put his stamina to test and jogged the final stretch to his destination. He arrived, flushed and sweating, just as Julian was leaving the barn he used as his studio. They shook hands formally, slapped each other ceremoniously on the shoulder and walked to the main house where Ginny was busy in the kitchen preparing coffee. Michael kissed her on both cheeks and sat down at the kitchen table. He never quite understood what Julian saw in her. Before Ginny, Julian had always fallen for the gypsy-like girls with wild flowing hair and long hippy dresses. Ginny was nothing like that, she was plain and simple, almost mousy. Yet, they loved each other and against all expectations had been together for more than five years.

'I bet you're wondering what I'm doing here,' Michael said after taking a sip of the bitter brew. 'Not really,' his brother replied, 'and I don't want to know either. You're always welcome here. You know that, you don't need a reason. Are you planning to stay?' 'I don't think so,' Michael said, 'I think I'll drive home before the end of the day.' 'Okay. Let's go to my studio. I'll show you what I'm up to and you can say hello to Alice,' Julian said, leading him out the door. 'Just one thing,' Michael said as they walked to the barn, 'don't tell anyone I've been here today. I'm sort of skipping class—a training day today; wasn't in the mood.' 'Sure!' Julian agreed. 'I'll also tell Ginny and Alice. I don't even know why you spend so much time playing that stupid game.'

After some hours, when Michael got back to the car, he realized how much he envied his brother. Julian never had to deal with the press breathing down his neck, he never worried about fame, fortune or prestige and was happy if he sold a painting now and again. 'You're super stressed,' Julian had remarked once during the day, 'you act as if your life is perfect, but you can't fool me, I can tell.' Michael laughed it off, reassuring him that nothing was wrong—he had never been happier. His brother had left it at that but was noticeably unconvinced. Michael wondered what he would do with the Hyundai. It had to disappear, that was a fact, but how? And where? The solution occurred to him a few miles beyond Cambridge.

When Michael had first arrived in London, he had shared an apartment with a teammate from Middlesex who was an avid fisherman. Michael had joined him a few times on fishing trips to his favourite spot; a lake in a deep gully just south of London surrounded on three sides by steep banks. The fisherman, after an unsuccessful career with the Panthers, had long since relocated to the minor league in Cumberland County—the remote, inhospitable north. But Michael remembered the spot all too well, they had spent hours there, fishing side-by-side. It was far from civilization in a conveniently wooded area.

Pleased with himself, he immediately called Tony. That he was asking his physiotherapy for help for the third time in 48 hours bothered him, but they were both in it so deep he could not imagine his friend would let him down now. Still. Tensely, he listened to the dull hum of the phone and was glad when Tony picked up. 'Where were you today?' was the first thing Tony asked. 'I showed up! Did you think I felt great? Everyone asked about you.' Michael afforded him some time to calm down before he asked, 'Can you help me again?' He expected Tony to protest, which he did, but eventually, he relented. 'I'll be there at 12,' he said, 'on the dot. I keep my appointments. You know that.'

Michael looked at his Rolex, it was almost six o'clock. He had time to kill before he could go to the lake. Perhaps the best plan would be to park the car in a quiet side street and catch a few hours of sleep. Vain as he was, he turned the rear-view mirror to check what the day had done to his looks; it was not good. When he turned the mirror back in its original position, he nearly had a heart attack. A police car was driving behind him. Michael hardly knew how to act. His first impulse was to step on the gas pedal and take off, but that was probably the stupidest thing he could do.

'When in doubt, sit still,' he thought. The car lingered behind him, like a cobra waiting for the perfect moment to attack. He suddenly didn't care anymore. Carine was dead, so was the child at the crosswalk, he'd have to pay. His life had gone to hell, he was done; it was over. Just then, the police car accelerated, overtook him and sped by. Gone in a flash. Michael could not even say he was relieved, he was beyond caring; it was all the same to him. He wearily took the next exit and drove the car into the first forest road he encountered. He set the alarm on his mobile phone, leaned his head against the window and fell asleep.

26

Tony

'WHAT THE HELL IS wrong with Michael?' Coach Allan's angry tone surprised Tony who was in the physiotherapy room attending to the severely injured Ed Morrison. It looked so bad that it took him a moment to answer. 'I don't know,' he said distracted. 'I haven't noticed anything out of the ordinary. But what we have here is a serious problem.' He pointed to the egg-like swell slowly taking shape on Ed's ankle. 'A torn ligament,' he continued. 'This will take a few months to heal.'

He looked at Ed's strained face—he looked as if he was about to cry. 'No World Cup for you, I'm afraid,' he said. 'I'm taking you to the hospital. We need a more precise diagnosis.' He saw that Allan had turned white. This was a setback they had not anticipated. Ed was a critical link in the England team and replacing him would not be easy. Allan left the room, cursing under his breath. Tony helped Ed off the table and handed him the crutch he had for emergencies like this. 'Brace yourself,' he said, 'the pain will subside, the first hour is always the worst.' Ed was crying now. 'Not now!' he moaned. 'I've been working for this for years!'

'This is a major setback,' Tony thought as he drove home from the hospital. Ed might not be of the same calibre as Michael

Cookson and James Hawkins, but he was still a vital force that could strike mercilessly at unexpected moments. It had been a strange experience—seeing a tough man like Ed diminished to a sobbing boy. 'We're all just vulnerable human beings,' he thought as he turned into his street. He hit the curb hard while parking and was sure of a flat tyre, but was lucky. Once inside, it took him a few moments to come to terms with his surroundings. What was he doing in this cold house?

He opened the refrigerator and saw that it was mostly empty. A bit of butter, a few eggs and half a carton of milk, two days past the expiry date—and that was pretty much it. His appetite had not improved since the morning, but he fried three eggs anyway and ate them reluctantly, struggling not to gag. As he shoved the last bite down his throat, his phone rang. 'Helen!' was the first thought that shot through his mind, but it was Michael.

His question was short and to the point. 'You can't desert me now,' he pleaded, 'I understand that you don't want to do this, but we're sort of in it together. And you're my friend.' Tony protested vehemently at first, but eventually gave in. After the call, Tony mulled over Michael's last words. Was he Michael's friend? Really? Did he actually have any friends? He sat on the sofa and watched the news without taking any of it in. 'Slowly sinking into the swamp,' he thought, 'where will this end?' He looked at the cigarette pack in front of him. One pack was all he allowed himself and it was still there. He tapped a cigarette out of the pack and lit it. Curiously enough, it did not make him nauseous.

Driving away from the curb he felt his Vauxhall swerve and knew he had a problem. A flat tyre after all. Fortunately, he had a half hour to spare, but it was doubtful he could change a tyre in that short a time—he wasn't what you'd call handy. 'I'll be there at 12,' he had told Michael, 'on the dot.' He knew where to find the spare tyre but the rest was a bit of a mystery to him. He fetched the manual from the glove compartment and moved underneath the street lamp to study it. The sudden barking behind him drew him out of his concentration. 'That fucking dog,' flashed through his mind. His nemesis, Alfie the Dobermann; he was terrified of that dog. The first time he had encountered the beast, he—dog hater par excellence—had attempted to pet him. The dog had promptly bit his right hand and he had the scar to prove it.

Neighbour Bob had apologized profusely: 'He never does that,' he'd insisted, but ever since, Tony had avoided that brute like the plague. And now, he was standing right behind him. 'Come here,' he heard Bob coax. 'Here, Alfie. Come to the boss.' Alfie growled viciously but reluctantly obeyed his owner. 'Can I help?' Bob said, 'I can fix that in no time.' Tony was tempted to decline, but a glance at his watch told him that would be foolish. 'Yes, please,' he said, 'that would be very kind of you.' 'Here, you take Alfie,' Bob said, 'he won't hurt you, honestly, I promise.'

Without waiting for Tony's answer, he thrust Alfie's leash in his hands and got to work. Within minutes, Bob replaced the flat tyre with the spare. All the while Tony stood like a pillar of salt, leash in hand, waiting for Alfie to attack. The relief he felt when he handed the leash back to Bob was immense. 'Thank you,' he said, 'really, thanks very much.' As he drove away, he realized he had waved goodbye to Bob—and to Alfie.

'Forty-five minutes,' Michael said, 'it won't take you longer than that.' 'Right, but you have to know where you're going,' Tony thought. His old Vauxhall did not have a built-in satnav and the satnav he had, had apparently never heard of the road Michael had mentioned. Fortunately, he had a good sense of direction and eventually arrived at the agreed upon spot. 'Stop two hundred yards down the dirt road and wait for me,' Michael had said. So he did.

Minutes passed and nothing happened. Just as he was about to venture further down the dirt road—perhaps he was in the wrong place—his mobile went off. 'I can't do it,' he heard Michael say. 'The front wheels are stuck in the dirt. The car won't budge. Do you have a shovel?' Michael told him exactly where he was and Tony set off, shovel in hand, to help him. After about a hundred yards down a narrow path, he saw a shadowy frame which looked like a car. As he drew closer, he discovered he was right. It was a small Hyundai hopelessly stuck in loose sand just off the edge of the gully, and next to it was Michael.

Although it was dark, Tony could see that Michael was in a state. His voice was shrill and he hopped erratically from foot to foot. 'Calm down,' Tony commanded, 'you'll screw everything up.' He plunged his shovel in the dirt and began digging out the front wheels. 'You've made a complete mess of things,' he said. 'They're seriously stuck; you've spun them in too deep.' It took half an hour before he had created enough space for traction. He estimated the distance to the steep bank, got behind the wheel and opened the windows. If he accelerated too much he and the car would disappear over the edge.

Slowly, he let the clutch up and gently pressed the accelerator pedal. His hard work had not been in vain. The Hyundai gradually climbed out of the hole and came to a halt at the edge of the gully. With cold sweat on his forehead, Tony got out and motioned to Michael to help with the final push. With their shoulders braced against the rear fenders they gave the final push. It was easy. The car tipped over the edge and seconds later it disappeared into the black water.

'They'll never find it,' Tony thought, 'unless someone points it out, no one will find this place.' He led Michael to the Vauxhall and because his companion seemed dazed, he opened the passenger door for him. 'Everything will be fine,' he said encouragingly as he settled himself behind the wheel, 'just stick to the story and nothing will happen.'

27

Dick

'IF IT WAS REALLY serious, something life threatening, they'd have called,' Julie said. 'It's really quite alright for you to go. I'll let you know as soon as I hear something.' She stood in the middle of a sunlit room, arms folded, legs slightly apart, in the tough pose she assumed when they discussed important issues. 'You'll never get a chance like this again,' she continued. 'Dick Anthony, investigative journalist, our man in the big bad world of cricket. Sounds like the title of an exciting boys' adventure book.'

Dick looked warmly at her. This was the woman he loved. This was the woman he would do anything for. 'Okay,' he said, 'only because you insist. But I'll be back the moment something's wrong. Rupert has let me rent a car, so the Fiesta is yours.' He walked over to her and hugged her tightly. He would miss her horribly. Since their marriage they had rarely spent a night apart. They hugged each other for a moment longer before he went upstairs to pack his bags. Tomorrow morning, he would be off.

He would astound the world with bold reports, background pieces and probing in-depth interviews. *The Northern Chronicle* would become the standard the national press would have to compete with. First, he would tackle the no-ball. It was just ridiculous how many wrongful no-ball decisions were made. How the hell was an umpire supposed to watch the arm and the foot of the bowler at the same time? They needed an electronic umpire— like the Hawk-Eye in tennis. Every time a bowler crossed the line a loud siren or horn should go off. That would nip all the suspicions in the bud.

Phil made a heroic effort. 'I did not know I had this hanging in the closet,' he laughed, 'but it seemed just the thing for our farewell dinner.' Dick burst out laughing when he saw his friend's dinner attire. The corn-yellow suit and bright red bow tie made him look a bit clownish. 'But it works,' Dick thought, 'he can actually pull it off!' They met at a restaurant in Finkle Street. Dick had never eaten there before but the 470 'excellents' on TripAdvisor had convinced him to try it.

'That you never filed charges against that bastard still surprises me,' Phil said as they toasted with a glass of expensive Château Sociando-Mallet—which Dick, of course, had let himself be talked into by the sommelier. 'That was a direct physical assault.'

Dick smiled sheepishly. Of course he had considered it, but Michael Cookson's punch hadn't been that bad and he couldn't be bothered with the rigmarole of pressing charges. And hadn't Michael Cookson always been his hero? 'Let's talk about something else,' he said, 'something more cheerful. Like a bloody murder for instance.' He knew that would get his friend going. Phil's crime-of-passion story was fascinating and occupied them well beyond dessert. 'Not to brag,' Phil said at the end, 'but I won that case. Against all odds. I even surprised myself.'

While he was busy telling one of his stories, he blatantly flirted with the charming, black-haired twenty-something waitress. He was a master at the art of flirting. It wasn't surprising that Giacomo Casanova's autobiography was one of his favourite reads. 'I hate to say it,' he often said, 'but I could still learn a lot from that old libertine.' And an eager student he was. Dick had never seen a girl blush as deeply as after one of Phil's almost obscene remarks—Phil at his absolute best. It surprised him they hadn't exchanged numbers yet—or maybe they had, you never knew with Phil. 'Good luck, old man,' Phil said as they left the restaurant at midnight, 'Take care of yourself. And maybe, just maybe, I'll visit!'

The image of Julie in the doorway with Ben, Harry and Owen clinging to her skirt stuck with him for miles. Not until he sped in the BMW past York did he allow the image to fade. 'It's time for the master plan,' he decided. He wished Joe was with him. Since his visit to the cemetery, he'd thought about his brother a lot. He could not shake his last image of Joe, covered in filth, a needle in his arm.

He had worried about him that day, more than usual. His brother had always descended into his own hell and had often slipped off the radar, and when he used to make contact, it had usually been to ask for money. But that time had been different; his silence had been ominous.

Dick remembered driving with a heavy heart and trembling hands to the address where he had expected to find his brother. It had been awful. The memory made Dick shudder. He put the sun visor down and tried to concentrate on traffic. 'Come on, Joe,' he whispered softly. 'How would you handle this?' He pictured Joe's lock of hair falling across his open face and missed him.

That he'd managed to get a room in Danubius Hotel in the middle of the tourist season was thanks to Rupert Thorpe. Rupert's extensive network stretched far, also in London, and luckily straight to the manager of the Danubius—Martin Walker. Rupert had subtly reminded him that he had saved him from a very sticky situation during their time at Oxford and that did the job. 'What exactly happened back then? Dick asked curiously, but Rupert was not forthcoming. 'Something with a young boy,' he murmured, 'Martin thought he was still at Eton.' Dick asked no further, too happy with the job that had fallen to him.

London traffic was horrible. Before he reached his hotel, he got stuck five times and five times he questioned his decision to come to London by car. On the other hand, he enjoyed the 240 miles he had driven in the luxurious BMW immensely. What a pleasure compared to the beat-up old Fiesta. With a smile he remembered how happy he and Julie had been when they had bought it—their first car! It had cost them more than three thousand pounds and the fact that they could afford it was mainly thanks to Julie's father—he had paid half.

Not that he was that well-off, but Julie was his princess and he would do anything for her, even sell off his stunning 1957 Morris Minor. In his heart, Dick had always been a bit envious of that beautiful dark green car and especially admired the grill at the back which had made it all the more special. His father-in-law had let him drive it the first time they had met—he had taken that as a good omen, surely if he had allowed him to drive the car, he would not have refused the hand of his daughter.

It took some time before he found a spot in the hotel's parking lot. Twenty-eight pounds per day—and that too on top of the steep room tariff—Rupert would not be thrilled. Dick laughed aloud at the thought of his editor's face when he would get the final bill. He took the two holdalls he had carefully packed from the boot, walked to the main entrance and checked in. In the lift, he stood next to a familiar face. The English star player James Hawkins was on his way to the fourth floor.

'Now or never,' Dick thought, conveniently forgetting the last time he had tried this. 'I'm Dick Anthony of *The Northern Chronicle*,' he said guardedly. 'Do you have time, today or tomorrow, for a short chat about the World Cup?' Hawkins did not seem surprised, he even smiled at him kindly. 'Actually, you need to run that by the team manager,' he said, 'but for such an important newspaper, I'm happy to make an exception. Tonight at half past ten in the lounge?' Dick beamed at him gratefully. He had his first interview. As easy as that. While unpacking his bags, he found two surprises. A bottle of his favourite whisky and a note penned in large ornate letters: I love you.

28

Vinoo

Vinoo had an awful itch, not just in the easy manageable areas, but all over his body. It was as if an entire army of biting ants were eating its way through his veins, leaving behind their prickly venom, driving him absolutely mad. After tossing and turning on his bed for an hour, he went to the bathroom to take an ice cold shower, hoping it would relieve the pain. But it didn't.

While he dried himself, he checked to see whether there were any marks on his skin, but there was nothing visible. Because he knew it would be difficult to sleep, he ambled to the window and stared out into the night. He thought of Dattu, he thought of his last night in Mumbai, but most of all, he thought about his dying grandfather.

He was at peace with the idea that, after a long and full life, the time had come for the old man.

But he would miss him sorely. He turned around and went to the desk in the corner of the room. For a while, he stared at the beautiful crest on the writing case the hotel provided for the guests. He remembered what Master Colah used to tell him, that if he didn't make it as a cricketer, he could always become a writer. His compositions were usually adorned with Master Colah's encouraging comments—'You know just how to set the scene', 'I love your sense of humour', 'You know exactly how to describe your characters'. Vinoo had been proud whenever he received them, even more than his achievements on the cricket field. Since he had made it in the real big world, his writing skills had remained unused. But now he felt a sudden urge. He took a pen and wrote:

'Dear Grandfather,

Although it is far past midnight, I can't sleep. You know that's not normal for me. As a child I slept the minute my head hit the pillow. But I'm digressing. I'm not writing just to gossip, I'm writing to tell you that I love you. So now I've said it. Since I've said goodbye, you have been in my thoughts constantly. I see you sitting on the chair nobody else is allowed to sit on, smoking a cigarette grandmother has forbidden you to smoke. I hear your stories about Ganish, who fell out of the tree and about the young Sachin who caught the ball just before it fell on the ground at Lord's. Sometimes you would tell me a story more than once, but I didn't mind. I loved them. Later you would come to the practice field to cheer me on. You were a grandfather and a father all in one. I remember how you mischievously said 'not out' after I made 502 runs. I say mischievously, because I did not understand the irony at the time. I was inconsolable. But you knew what you were doing. I became even more fanatical.'

The knock on the door surprised him. It took him a few seconds to get his bearings. 'Who could it be? Who would dare to disturb him at this ungodly hour?' Remembering his last night in Mumbai, he looked around for something to arm himself with, but realized that he wouldn't stand a chance against someone carrying a gun or a knife. 'It's time to face your fears,' the little voice inside him whispered. 'No one scares the great Vinoo Ramji. He has fought tougher battles'. He quickly pulled open the door making sure he could get away if anyone tried to pounce on him. It was quiet in the hallway. He slowly went out, prepared for an unexpected attack. But he was alone.

Not for long. Three rooms down the door opened and an old, bent woman came out and made her way slowly to the elevator. She did not turn around. It seemed unlikely that she had knocked on his door. Having checked the hallway once again, he went back to his room.

'I became even more fanatical.' It had been his last sentence. His inspiration was gone. He opened the minibar and took out the three miniature whisky bottles. 'If Mother Nature doesn't work, I might as well help her along a bit,' he sighed. He usually didn't drink alcohol, but now he finished the bottles one by one and went to bed. After a few minutes, he felt his eyelids getting heavier.

Although he had only slept a few hours, he felt better than expected when he got up at seven o'clock. The itch had subsided and he didn't have a hangover. The scratch marks on his arms, legs and body were silent reminders of the tortuous night he had endured. Naked, in front of the mirror after his shower, it was clear how battered he had been.

While dressing, he noticed the unfinished letter to his grandfather. He crumpled it up and threw it into the waste basket, but quickly picked it up again to tear it into little pieces. This was nobody's business; it was something between himself and his grandfather. He deserved better. With a quiet nod, he promised himself to make an effort to put his love for his grandfather into words.

29

Allan

ALLAN COULD NOT BELIEVE his eyes. In his entire cricket career, he had never seen anything so idiotic. Returning home from dinner at the Palomar—which had ended in silence—Valerie moved into the living room to watch a late soap, while Alan settled himself in his study to watch the recorded match between Australia and Lancashire. The copious amount of alcohol he had consumed to get him through dinner had made him sleepy; but not sleepy enough to miss the bizarre incident.

Aussie bowler Peter Owen came charging, produced a ripper and made the stumps fly about fifty feet towards the wicketkeeper. Allan waited for the batsman to leave the field, but he remained standing at the wicket; the umpire's arm had gone up. No-ball. No wicket with a ripper like that! Everyone seemed to accept the umpire's ruling until the televised replay showed the close-up of the bowler's foot. It had landed precisely *on* and not *over* the line. Because the images were also shown on the screens at Old Trafford, Allan noted he was not the only one speechless.

The entire stadium was stupefied. The only person who didn't blink an eye was the umpire himself. The next over, he missed a definite No-ball and five more after that! 'That was his last game,'

Allan thought to himself, 'but who knows, maybe he's set for life.' He walked to the living room for a whisky to wash away the absurd events in Manchester and found Valerie half-undressed on the sofa. 'You've been without so long,' she whispered seductively. 'You must be longing for me.' Allan did not know how to respond, but was saved by the shrill sound of the doorbell.

The first thing Allan noticed about the man in the doorway was the deep horizontal cleft carved centrally in his forehead. And then his raincoat; an old gaberdine in the style of a bygone era. 'My name is Donald,' the man said, 'my last name, and as a matter of fact, it is also my first name,' he smiled mildly. 'I'm Detective Inspector Donald of Scotland Yard. May I come in? It's a delicate matter.' Allan thought of the scantily clad Valerie and hesitated. 'It won't take long,' the man insisted, 'no more than ten minutes.' Allan stepped back and made room for the man to pass and from the corner of his eye, he saw Valerie, with her dress under her arm, sprint up the stairs.

'Please, follow me,' he said as he led the way to the living room. 'Can I pour you a drink?'

'No, thank you,' said D.I. Donald, 'as I said, I'll just take a moment.'

Allan's mind was in overdrive now. What could a Scotland Yard D.I. possibly want from him? He poured the whisky that he had promised himself and turned to the D.I.

'It's not about you,' the man said, 'but someone you know well. It's Michael Cookson actually.'

'Really? What about him?' Allan asked, 'As far as I know, he is ill at home, he called in sick this morning with abdominal pain, just before training.'

'Perhaps,' the man said, 'but according to my information, he was involved in a traffic accident this morning, in Cambridge. A serious traffic accident, I might add, a hit-and-run. The Hyundai involved is registered to him.'

Allan felt some relief. 'That may be,' he said, 'but that's his girlfriend Carine's car, not Michael's; he drives a Jaguar, he's practically married to it. Not a chance he would drive a little Korean number, far below his standard.' D.I. Donald appeared a bit puzzled. 'The woman whose daughter was seriously injured is almost certain that a man was driving,' he said after a brief pause, 'and the man who witnessed the incident agrees.'

Allan's relief gave way to anxiety. '*Almost*,' he repeated, '*almost* means they could be mistaken.'

'Yes, that's possible,' DI Donald said, his cleft starting to look like the Grand Canyon, 'but I would still like to speak to Mr Cookson and his girlfriend. The problem is I can't seem to get a hold of either. I've tried Mr. Cookson's address a few times, but he doesn't seem to be at home, even though his Jaguar is parked out front.'

'He'll probably be in bed,' Allan said. 'With his earplugs in. If you have the stomach flu you really want to be left alone.'

'And his girlfriend?' D.I. Donald asked, 'I imagine she would be at home?'

'Oh Carine,' Allan said, 'she's home sometimes and sometimes she's not, if you know what I mean.'

'I'm afraid I don't,' said D.I. Donald, 'please explain.' Allan cursed his big mouth. 'She's out a lot,' he said curtly, 'that's really all I have to say.'

'Maybe you could call them for me,' asked D.I. Donald, 'then they can speak for themselves.'

'Of course,' said Allan, 'my pleasure.'

He went to his study to get his iPhone. Returning to the living room, he called Michael, then Carine—both calls went unanswered. He gave D.I. Donald their numbers and accompanied him to the front door. As he left, D.I. Donald handed him his card, 'Just in case'.

The Detective Inspector's visit had sobered him up. Something was terribly wrong, he could feel it. After brooding over the visit for several minutes, he informed Valerie that he had to leave because of an emergency. Not waiting for a reply, he hurried to his Mercedes— the fancy car Valerie had urged him to buy that he actually hated; too big, too fast. He manoeuvred carefully through the subdued night traffic. Lost in thought, he didn't notice the police roadblock until it was too late—alcohol control. He tried to remember when he had his last drink and concluded this would be a toss-up. 'Why the hell didn't I take a cab?' he reprimanded himself. But he had no time to reflect as a policewoman with a black mole on the corner of her mouth, a sagging under-chin but a provocatively sexy voice, presented him a breathalyser.

'Blow hard,' she said, 'don't try to hold back.' As she held his fate in her hands, he stared through the windshield. 'This would make for interesting headlines,' he thought. 'You've been drinking,' the provocative voice reported, 'but you're within legal limits. I'd be careful from now on. But you're good to go, have a good evening.' He wiped the perspiration from his brow, slowly let the clutch up and turned the corner. He had been right, it had been a toss-up. Like someone who'd just passed the driving exam, he crawled the final distance, wary of attracting attention.

Michael's house was pitch-black except for a dim red flicker vaguely visible behind the curtain. Allan suspected a candle. He rang the doorbell, there was no response. He stood back and looked at the window. He saw the curtain move slightly, followed by the sound of footsteps. A light switched on in the hallway and then the door opened. Allan was taken aback. Michael hadn't looked particularly fit at training, but he looked ten times worse now. He had clearly not shaved and the black stubble on his pale cheeks made him look outright sinister. 'I know it's late,' Allan said, 'but can I come in?' Michael did not answer, and led him into the candlelit living room. He noticed the rancid smell of cigarettes and a recently opened bottle of whisky on the table.

'You want a shot?' Michael asked him.

'Not right now,' Allan said. 'I just barely passed an alcohol test. But let's get to the point, where were you today?' Michael looked at him, struggling to focus. 'Here and there,' he said. 'I told you this morning my stomach was a mess, but actually I was upset because Carine has left me. When I woke up this morning, I noticed that she'd only been home to leave a note on the kitchen counter. She's definitely gone; she's left me. I suspected she had a lover, but we had an open relationship so I didn't think much of it. It came as a bit of shock.' He lit a cigarette and inhaled deeply.

Allan was repulsed. 'A policeman was at my door this evening,' he said. 'He said Carine's Hyundai was involved in a hit-and-run in Cambridge this morning. Do you know anything about that?'

Michael looked at him impassively, 'No,' he said, 'I feel bad for her, but I can't help you.'

'And you have no idea who the man behind the wheel was?' Allan asked, looking intently at Michael. But he didn't flinch. 'No,' he said, 'I spent the entire day sitting on the banks of the Thames with a bottle of whisky, but I think that's obvious. I fell asleep when I got home and just woke up an hour ago.'

'You look like shit,' Allan said, 'I'm not used to seeing you like this. Was your phone off all day?'

'I threw it in the river,' Michael, said, 'along with the damn note. I wanted nothing to do with anyone today. Strange but true, I even surprised myself, but that's just the way it is.' Allan noted that

Michael seemed to become himself as the conversation progressed.

'Right, I'm off,' he said. 'You can expect a visitor tomorrow; so be prepared.' Alan got up, grabbed Michael by the arm and looked him straight in his eyes, 'Take care of yourself,' he said, 'England needs you.'

30

Mohammed

Bᴀᴄᴋ ɪɴ ʜɪs ʜᴏᴛᴇʟ room Mohammed called Aslam Ali. 'You've done well,' he said, 'how about two thousand pounds extra per no-ball?' By the silence on the other end he deduced Aslam was impressed. 'I'll call you soon,' he added, crankier than intended, 'sleep well and dream about all the things you'll be able to afford soon.' Reluctant to spend the rest of the evening in his room, he took the elevator down to the bar to once again inspect the pictures of his heroes. After a long look at the legendary Richie Benaud, he left the hotel. It had been a warm day, at least seventy degrees, but it was chilly now. Shivering in his thin linen jacket Mohammed decided to take a walk.

To his left he noticed the bright sign of Lord's Pharmacy shining in the dusk. From the corner of his eye he saw the young woman who had helped him, working the evening shift. Like a peeping Tom, he posted himself at the window and peered inside. She was preoccupied with a man at the counter, the only customer in the pharmacy. He wore faded, sagging sweatpants and a large bag of medicine was perched on the counter in front of him. Apparently, he needed a detailed explanation, because she was busy with him for several long minutes at various intervals. Each time he seemed satisfied with her explanation, made his way to leave the pharmacy, but only to turn back, retrace his steps to the counter and ask more questions. It seemed like a never-ending pageant, but finally he was satisfied and left for good.

Mohammed did not hesitate even for a second and went inside. The young woman had disappeared into the backroom giving him time to think of an opening line. When at last she reappeared and noticed him, she asked: 'How may I help you?' Mohammed's heart sank. Apparently, he had not made much of an impression on her. 'Don't you recognize me?' he asked shyly, 'You recently helped me.' Her face lit up, 'Oh yes!' she exclaimed, 'You were the nauseous man.'

Mohammed heard the door behind him open and grit his teeth; a tic in times of stress. The last thing he need, now was to be interrupted. By the exasperated look on her face he knew who it was. He turned and looked icily at the man in the faded sweatpants. 'I think you've had more than enough service,' he said as he coolly grabbed him by the throat and squeezed him until the man turned purple. 'Now leave,' he continued, relaxing his grip. 'And do the world a favour; swallow the entire contents of your bag at once. Get it over with.'

The man, who had a remarkably piggish face, looked stunned. He was about to say something but thought better of it as Mohammed opened the door and pushed him forcefully out on the street, where he landed, tripping and stumbling to gain his balance. 'Let him open his own pharmacy,' he said as he turned back to the woman. To his delight, she seemed amused rather than shocked. 'It's a daily ritual,' she said, 'the doctors have given up on him and prescribe whatever he asks for. It's a miracle he's still alive. You'll never meet a bigger hypochondriac.'

As she spoke Mohammed felt an unfamiliar sensation. He

looked at her and was struck by how beautiful she was. He thought of the vow of chastity his boss Hussain demanded of him and decided those days were over.

'Hello! You seem to have disappeared,' the woman said with an amused smile, 'am I not interesting enough for you?' Mohammed blushed. But he wasn't going to allow this opportunity to slip through his fingers.

'You interest me very much,' he said regaining his composure, 'I was thinking of that fool just now.' The woman pushed her headscarf back exposing her thick black sensuous hair. Mohammed struggled to breathe. 'I think you are from Pakistan,' he said after a few seconds, 'from where exactly, if I may ask?'

'I've heard better lines than that before,' she said, now smiling brightly, 'but you're right. I'm from Islamabad.'

Mohammed could kick himself. Here he had a chance to interact with this amazing women and he was fumbling like a schoolboy.

'Sorry,' he said, 'you're just so beautiful. And I'm not myself at the moment. Would you like to have dinner with me?'

'My name is Aneesha, by the way,' she said, 'and yes, I'd like to have dinner with you. I rather like awkward men.'

Mohammed wanted to leap across the counter and embrace her but instead, he formally asked, 'When?' 'Why don't you suggest a date?'

She said, 'Of course, I'm horribly busy, but I may have a hole in my schedule somewhere.' Ironically intended or not, her remark did not help boost Mohammed's confidence.

'Tomorrow night?' he asked hopefully.

'Alright,' she said, 'my shift ends at seven. Pick me up here?' A nod was all Mohammed could manage. He was the happiest man on earth.

The curly blonde man from the tour was in the lounge and was wrapped in deep conversation with the English batsman James Hawkins. Mohammed was surprised to see that his nose looked fairly normal considering the punch Michael Cookson had landed on it. The two seemed to get on so well that he felt a stab of jealousy shoot through him. James Hawkins was his target, he must not forget that. He sat down at the bar across from the portrait of Ian Botham and thought of his own mullet that used to grow down the back of his neck years ago; it was hard to imagine those days.

As he was Muslim he had always stayed away from alcohol, but after meeting Aneesha he had the urge to get drunk. 'A Johnny Walker,' he said, ordering the only brand he could think of. 'With ice,' he added, because he thought it sounded cool. The first sip burned its way down his throat, the second went smoother and by the third, he was hooked. He felt fantastic. A night like this came once in a lifetime. He was on top of the world. He got up to urinate and he realized he could barely stand. A nagging voice told him he had drank enough; he was about to make a staggering fool of himself. In the men's room he completely missed the urinal, creating a yellow-brown puddle at his feet. He looked at it smiling. Tomorrow he was having dinner with Aneesha.

Leaving the bar, he banged awkwardly against James Hawkins' chair. He mumbled an apology and stumbled into the lobby. Back in his room, he lay on the bed and watched the ceiling reel slowly towards him. Thinking of Aneesha, he reached for his penis but couldn't bring it to life. He felt a strong urge to vomit, but no matter how deep he stuck his finger down his throat, nothing came out.

31

Dick

Dɪᴄᴋ ʜᴀʀᴅʟʏ ᴇᴠᴇʀ ᴘʀᴇᴘᴀʀᴇᴅ for the interviews he did for *The Northern Chronicle*. Most of the locals were usually so flattered they were being interviewed that they spilled the beans in no time. When he had started out as a rookie reporter, he used to tape every interview, but he gave that up as soon as he realized he could rarely make heads or tails of the gibberish he had recorded. Nothing was more effective than a good old-fashioned notebook and a few jotted keywords—sufficient for an article of any length. But this was different, a completely different kettle of fish. Preparation was vital.

His conversation with James Hawkins had to deliver the content for his first background piece. That was obvious. Seated at the window of his hotel room, overlooking a railroad track with an antique locomotive, he looked at the website on his iPad. James Hawkins had had a tough life; absentee father, mother working as a night nurse, only child, no genius at school, but a fanatic when it came to sports. As a soccer player, he could arguably have made it to the Premier League, but unlike many of his classmates, he chose cricket. This was largely due to Colin Milburn, the barrel-chested hard hitter.

Knowing he was a cricket fan, his English teacher had lent

him a Milburn biography and it changed his life. The cricket hero of yesteryear became his role model. Of course Dick knew Hawkins was no Colin Milburn, but he had witnessed some of Milburn's bravado in Hawkins when he had watched him play Northamptonshire against Durham at Chester-le-Street. He had carried his bat gloriously through the innings while his teammates' wickets fell one by one. He had recently married a soap opera star, at first glance, a bit of a bimbo; not someone Dick had pictured James with.

Dick checked a few more sites, kept his tablet aside and called Julie. 'How wonderful to hear your beautiful voice,' he said gallantly, 'how's my fair lady?' But his light-heartedness was lost on her.

'Not great, I'm in a funk,' she said in a teary voice, 'I get the results tomorrow.'

Dick immediately felt guilty. 'Shall I come home?' he said. 'I can be there in a few hours.'

But Julie quickly recovered, 'I'm overreacting,' she said, 'it's probably nothing. You stay put in London. How's your article coming?'

'Tonight will be important,' Dick replied, 'I have my first interview. Wish me luck.'

The lounge was crowded. Dick made his way between the tables scouring the room for James Hawkins. He spotted him a few seconds later. James was sitting comfortably in a chair and was sipping on a glass of orange juice. He was not the only cricketer relaxing, Dick saw several familiar faces around the room.

James Hawkins was not a man for ceremonies, 'Ask away,' he said, 'I am at your disposal. What are you drinking?'

Dick, wanting to stay alert, ordered mineral water and asked his first question. James proved to be an ideal conversationalist and that he knew a thing or two about cricket history was an extra bonus.

When Colin Milburn was mentioned, his eyes lit up. 'He was dead before I was born,' he said, 'a heart attack at 48. But he did live life to the fullest. There's a reason they called him "Ollie", nicknamed after the tubby Oliver Hardy. But what a player, what zest!'

Dick was thrilled to have stumbled on their common interest in the rich history of cricket, full of amazing anecdotes. They were chatting like old friends. In his enthusiasm he forgot to take notes but was sure that he would remember the conversation verbatim. At eleven o'clock, he suddenly remembered the purpose of the evening and got back to the point. 'Just a few more questions,' he said. 'What do you think of the English team being the top favourite when it comes to winning?'

'According to everyone we'll win the championship,' James said, 'and we obviously have a very strong team. But you never know.' It was a cliché answer and his wandering gaze indicated that he would speak no more on that question.

'Ever noticed any signs of match-fixing? Have you ever been approached yourself?' Dick asked.

James Hawkins did not seem shocked by the blunt question. 'Of course, it happens. It does in all sports. It involves big money. I myself have never been tempted. Although,' he pointed to a Pakistani sipping whisky at the bar, 'that is one curious devil, a real journalist. He invited me to have dinner with him. Seemed very eager for any news about our team. But maybe it's nothing.'

'And what about the no-balls?' Dick asked, 'In Taunton, for example, on the first, third and fifth ball of the over. Wasn't that a bit suspicious?'

'Did seem a bit iffy,' James replied, 'but what can you do?

This enraged Dick. 'Surely in this day and age, with all the technology available, it should be possible do something about that!' he exclaimed. 'A siren or horn or something can indicate when a bowler crosses the line? Put an end to all the needless discussions.'

James laughed, 'Well, you're certainly in the right industry, you have a newspaper at your disposal. Publish it,' he said, 'get it off your chest. You can dedicate a column to it.'

Dick suddenly felt uncomfortable and abruptly changed the subject. 'I've read that the players and staff who live in London will only join the team early next week. Is that true and if so, how do you feel about that?' he asked to wind up the interview. 'No comments,' was all he got in reply.

James might have said more had the Pakistani from the bar not bumped into James' chair as he lurched to the exit. 'What a fitting end,' he remarked, 'I think I'll call it a night.' Almost like friends they shook hands and James walked towards the elevator. Dick ordered a well-deserved gin and tonic and consulted his notebook. It was empty.

The opening sentence—always one of his strongest points—was just not coming to him this time. After deleting the tenth attempt he was sure it was not going to come to him that night. He stood by the window and thought of the past few days. The vulnerability he always felt when he was away from Julie frightened him. What if something was wrong? What if cancer slowly destroyed her body? What if she died? He stared at his reflection in the window, and saw an old, sombre face. Of course he should have stayed at home. Of course he should not have given in to her insistence. He was a self-centred, disgusting bastard. He picked up his phone off the nightstand and saw that he had a text message. 'I'm going to sleep. Lots of love. Till tomorrow,' it read.

In other words—Do Not Disturb. Just as he put the phone down, it rang. 'Good evening, or good night actually,' said Phil, 'may I bother you at this ungodly hour with a few important announcements?'

'And what if I say no?' Dick joked, happy to hear a familiar voice. 'What's on your mind?'

'Do you remember Vivian?' Phil asked, 'The girl who served us in the Rustique?'

Dick had to think twice. 'Yes!' he said, 'That ugly one with the greasy scarecrow yellow hair, blackheads on her forehead and a sagging butt.' It was Phil's turn to be quiet for a while.

'Ha, ha, very funny,' Phil eventually said, 'but all jokes aside, what did you think of her?'

'Too young for you in any case,' Dick said.

'When I ran into her on my way to the washroom, she told me in passing that she had never seen such an idiotic suit,' Phil retaliated.

Dick did not respond to Phil and the silence continued for several long seconds. 'What's wrong with you?' Phil said. 'Am I speaking to the right person?'

'Of course, sorry,' Dick said, 'you caught me in one of my morose moods. I'm very happy you called. Please, go on.'

'You, of course, did not notice,' Phil continued, 'but Vivian and I fell for each other like a ton of bricks. She loves spiritual, extravagant and sexy men. Age is not an issue for her. Sex is. She knows everything about sex. I could learn a lot from her.'

'Could?' Dick interjected.

'Yes, could,' said Phil, 'we hit it off that first evening. And I can talk to her, even though she didn't finish secondary school. I think I'll stay with her. I can see myself in a morganatic marriage. It's time I settle down.'

'Congratulations,' Dick said, 'she sounds like a real winner!'

When their conversation ended, it was two in the morning. Dick sat down to work. Phil, as usual, had inspired him. The first sentence came, and the rest followed. Two hours later, he had his first rough draft and he set off to bed. 'Tomorrow, 'I'll show Rupert what's what. *The Northern Chronicle* will astonish the world.'

32

Allan

ALLAN WAS DRIVING LIKE an old maid—a sure-shot way to draw the attention of any passing police car. He increased his speed to meet the maximum speed limit and let his thoughts drift back to his conversation with Michael. His team captain's strange behaviour bothered him. Of course Carine could have run off with a lover, but the way Michael told the story seemed too calculated—almost robotic. The emotions Michael claimed to feel were certainly not discernible. But maybe that's just the way he was. In the short time Allan had known him, he had seen him seduce at least a dozen beautiful women. Carine never seemed to notice, or she pretended not to. It was possible that Michael was devastated, that this time, he was the deceived party.

The light in the bedroom was still on. Not surprising, he knew Valerie couldn't sleep if she hadn't read a good number of pages of her beloved Jackie Collins. He prided himself on the fact that he had not read a single book since middle school. 'All fabricated nonsense,' he often said. 'I deal with the real world.' Yet, sometimes he was jealous of someone like the hard-hitting batsman Ed Morrison who spent every free moment with a book in a corner, completely cut off from the world. The thought of one of his favourite players made him curse. His injury was a major setback.

Parallel parking had never been his strong point, but he made a complete mess of it now. After several failed attempts, he was relieved when he finally managed to squeeze his car in a spot, although it was nearly two feet from the curb. In the living room, a candle was still burning, casting a ghostly shadow on the walls. Allan was wide awake and felt no urge to go to bed. He turned on the TV, zapped through the channels, but nothing caught his interest.

Just as he decided he might as well join Valerie, his phone rang. 'Out and about so late?' said the voice he now knew all too well. 'Did your captain need to be tucked in? Couldn't fall asleep without holding your hand? But I understand, he can use all the help he can get in these difficult times.'

'What?' Allan blurted, 'What are you talking about? Who is this?' But there was no reply. He stared at the phone clenched in his hand. What the hell did this mean? Michael needed help because Carine had left him? Was there more to it? And how did the man get this information? He couldn't get answers from the man with the deep voice—that coward always hid behind an unknown number. For a moment he was tempted to call Michael, but then he thought better of it and went upstairs.

Valerie had put her book on the bedside table and was sitting up in bed, her breasts bared. She threw the duvet back and beckoned invitingly. Strangely enough, Allan didn't feel the reluctance he usually did before he surrendered to her. This time, he felt pure lust. He quickly took off his clothes and fell clumsily on the bed. 'I've rarely seen you that excited,' Valerie laughed with a look undoubtedly meant to be enticing, but all Allan saw was a smirk. Lovemaking with Valerie was usually short-lived, as it was now. 'You might as well do it with an inflatable doll,' she said with a sigh after he rolled off her. Allan felt too embarrassed to answer.

The whirlwind in his head was a sign of a sure-shot insomnia, but the delayed reaction to the alcohol and the rollercoaster ride of the past few hours knocked him out in a heartbeat. When the urge to urinate woke him up at five o'clock, he felt as if he'd had a full night's sleep. With some compassion, he looked down at Valerie, snoring with her mouth open, and decided to go downstairs. In the kitchen, he made a cup of strong coffee, went outside and sat at the garden table on the terrace. The birds had started chirping. He watched one land on the dew-covered lawn. Seemingly unhappy on the lawn, the bird shot back up in the air within seconds, as if launched by a missile. After half an hour, he began feeling cold and promptly went back inside.

The Lord's Tavern was busier than the last time he had been there. As Allan waited for Brian Jameson to arrive he watched a tennis match on the TV in the corner, but the two ladies playing moon balls couldn't really grab his attention. Luckily, he saw the portly figure of the chairman of the English Cricket Board appear between the tables. Allan sat up, bracing himself for the usual blow on his shoulder, but Brian chose a handshake, crushing Allan's bones in the process.

Unlike what they had ordered a few days ago, they both chose a toasted sandwich. 'Bad news about Ed, eh! Who is going to replace him?' Brian—not one to waste any time and always quick to strike a nerve. 'I have a name in mind,' he continued, 'but the decision is yours of course.'

'Asshole,' thought Alan, 'you obviously want to have your way and push that wimp Maurice Flanagan, the league's little darling boy, to the top of the list.'

'Cat got your tongue?' Brian asked, 'Did I say something wrong?'

'No, of course not,' Allan said. 'I'm just considering the options.

Actually, I'm not even sure I will call up a replacement.'

'I most certainly would,' Brian was quick to reply, 'and if I were you, I would immediately opt for Maurice Flanagan. He's the biggest upcoming talent we have. He still lacks toughness, but a tournament like this can fix that in no time.'

'He's one of the possibilities,' Allan said as neutrally as possible, 'but as I said, I'm still weighing the options.'

'Now on another subject,' Brian said, 'I hear from various sources that Michael looks appalling these days. What's wrong with him?'

'It's just high time he joins the team,' Allan said. 'All that spare time is not good for him. But I assure you, I'll have him back on track before you know it.' Brian gazed at him thoughtfully for a moment, and then, somewhat awkwardly, attacked the oversized toasted sandwich. 'Maurice Flanagan,' he said with his mouth full. 'I would definitely select him.'

33

Michael

HE WOULDN'T BE ABLE to get out of it today, he couldn't milk his 'stomach flu' forever. Michael knew training on an empty stomach was a bad idea, so he poured a dash of milk over a bowl of cornflakes and ate his breakfast half-heartedly. He had never had heartburns in his life—until now. The burning acid reflux bubbled up in his oesophagus just seconds after his meal. He rinsed his mouth with water extensively, but couldn't get rid of the horrible taste. 'What a beginning to a day,' he grumbled, 'this should be fun.'

As he went upstairs to pack his bag, the doorbell rang. His first impulse was to not answer it, but realizing he couldn't hide forever, he retraced his steps and headed for the door. Through the smoked glass he saw a bent silhouette listening at the door as if trying to ascertain if anyone was home.

'D.I. Donald,' the man said after Michael opened the door, 'I tried to call to tell you I was coming, but I couldn't get a hold of you. And yesterday you weren't home either. I got your number from Allan Moorcombe, who also tried to call you. It seemed you had vanished from the face of the earth!'

'I suppose in a way I had,' Michael said as he stared with fascination at the man's forehead. 'But what did you want to speak to me about?'

'Well, it's not something I'd care to discuss out here on the sidewalk,' said D.I. Donald. 'May I come in?' The blood rushed to his Michael's cheeks. That was his mistake. 'Of course,' he said, a little faster than intended, 'please follow me, we'll go to the living room.'

To avoid a second mistake, Michael, with exaggerated politeness, invited D.I. Donald to take a seat in his favourite club chair while he sat on the sofa. 'I'll keep it brief,' the policeman said as he pulled out a small black notebook. 'Where were you yesterday morning around half past twelve?'

Michael struggled to keep his emotions in check, barely managing to stay calm. 'I'm not exactly sure where I was,' he said. 'I was quite upset by the fact that my girlfriend had left me. She broke up rather abruptly.'

'Sorry to hear that,' D.I. Donald said with a Buster Keaton straight face, 'did you perhaps drive her car to Cambridge?'

Michael realized his next answer was crucial. 'No,' he said firmly, 'I didn't. I do remember going to a quiet spot along the Thames at some point, to drown my grief with a bottle of whisky. I think the result is probably still visible?'

D.I. Donald remained stoic. 'Perhaps you know the man who was driving your ex-girlfriend's Hyundai?' he asked, 'That car caused a serious accident yesterday.'

Michael grabbed the lifeline extended to him with both hands. 'No, I don't,' he said, 'Carine wasn't very forthcoming about her new boyfriend.'

For the first time, D.I. Donald showed a glimpse of emotion. 'New boyfriend?' he asked. 'You hadn't mentioned that.'

'Well, I'd only just heard about him myself the last time we spoke,' Michael said, 'I wasn't too worried. He wasn't the first. We did genuinely care for each other, but in that aspect, we let each other free. Usually, they were like ships passing in the night. But this last one was apparently more than that. She was quite taken with him, I did realize that.'

'Did anyone see you sitting by the Thames?' asked D.I .Donald while plucking at a piece of cotton stuck to a shaving wound on his cheek.

'I don't think so,' Michael answered. 'I needed to be alone. So I found a spot where nobody could see me.'

'Have you been in touch with your girlfriend since she left?' asked D.I. Donald who now had a thick drop of blood running down his cheek. 'Has she called you? Or contacted you in any way?'

Michael handed his guest a tissue from a big box on the table. 'No, not a word,' he said, 'not a sign. You're probably expecting to hear a caring goodbye or a final bit of consolation, but that's not Carine. Once she's made up her mind, it's done. Out of sight, out of mind. I'll never hear from her again. I'm sure.'

D.I. Donald silently looked at him for a while. 'Disappeared into thin air,' he commented, 'disappeared without a trace. I suppose you'll let me know immediately in the unlikely event you do hear from her? Nice car, by the way, your Jaguar. Have you had it for long?'

Michael was surprised by the sudden change of topic and didn't quite know how to respond. 'Just a year,' he said, after a long silence. 'It is an E-type 1969, a special little car.'

D.I. Donald remained silent, nodding in agreement. He stood up, buttoned up his old-fashioned raincoat and walked to the door.

'I'll be in touch,' he said, turning around. 'Your ex-girlfriend will surely turn up somewhere. Then we can compare your stories.'

Michael hated the rain. On those inert afternoons when thick dark rain clouds spewed out endless streams of water making cricket impossible, he couldn't concentrate on card games or check the stock market like the rest of his teammates did to kill time. On the contrary, he checked the skies every five minutes looking for some hope in the grey mass, usually in vain. After a day like that, he was insufferable, and it looked like it was one of those days. When he closed the door behind him, he saw the violent downpour of rain ricochet off the asphalt. It was definitely another one of those days.

That his Jaguar took five attempts to come back to life didn't help his mood. His trusted car, which never let him down, now seemed bedevilled. He finally drove off and carefully manoeuvred through traffic. As his windshield wipers could hardly manage the torrent of water he almost missed a van.

Quietly cursing, he drove into the gates of Lord's. The first thing he saw when he got out of his car was the tall figure of Tony surrounded by a group of players all vying for his attention. His partner in crime nodded to him and returned his attention to his clients. It was always a competition—who would be first in line to receive his magical treatment. In the dressing room, he ran into Allan.

'Well?' he asked, ignoring the others. 'Did you have any interesting visitors?'

'Yes, I did have a visitor,' Michael said. 'But interesting?'

He gave Allan a smile and kept quiet.

34

Vinoo

His eyes were uncontrollably drawn to his navel, and of course to the finger he repeatedly poked in it. Dattu had no inhibitions and poked to his heart's content. This time his shirt exposed a roll of fat, flagrantly bulging over his belt. He had literally begged Vinoo, requesting him for a bit of his time, until Vinoo had finally caved in. But now, as they sat opposite each other, Dattu was substantially less servile, and the urgency of his pleas was gone. After his navel-poking exercises he shifted his attention to his beard, making ringlets with his fat finger.

'You misunderstood me,' he said after a while. 'You suspect me of false intentions. I'm a bit disappointed. We've never dealt with each other that way.'

Vinoo listened in silence. He wasn't sure what to make of the situation. Here he was sitting across a man who wanted something from him, something he would never give him. How could they ever get back to the way it used to be? 'It's just harmless information,' he heard Dattu say as he leaned forward conspiratorially. Vinoo involuntarily recoiled, repulsed as he was by the greasy beard and the finger that had just poked his grimy navel. 'Innocent information,' Dattu repeated. 'Just as innocent as the information

I could give Aasia about your relationship with Deepika.'

Suddenly, Vinoo was completely focused. This was his big secret. Even Vijay knew nothing about it. It was something between him and Deepika, something that nothing and no one could tarnish. 'What you get up to in room 303 of the Vivanta is of course harmless,' Dattu said. 'Playing house, for example. Surely there is no harm in it.' His sarcasm was palatable and his face was so close Vinoo could smell raw onions in his breath. He was sweating profusely now and wished he was anywhere but in the lobby of the Hilton, far away from his tormentor.

'But however innocent your games may be, I've captured them with my camera,' Dattu said, 'I believe they'll surprise Aasia. I hear she can be rather jealous. And I know, of course, plenty of newspapers would feast on this story. I can see the headlines now.' Vinoo felt himself on the verge of an outburst, but he controlled himself.

'What do you want?' he said coldly when he had regained control on his temper. 'What are your filthy little plans?'

'My plans are not filthy at all,' Dattu said. 'As I said, just a bit of harmless information. Preferably just before a match.' He got up and tried, in vain, to stuff his shirt into his pants.

'The last time we spoke, you said something about danger in the streets. What did you mean?' Vinoo asked, annoyed with himself that he had not asked the question sooner, but Dattu had gotten up and had quickly marched out of the lobby.

'What was that all about? What did that greaseball want?' Vijay looked at him with his bulging eyes.

'Oh nothing,' Vinoo said. 'He was a little drunk, I think he's gone to sleep it off.' Vijay looked doubtful but did not persist.

'Want to play?' he asked. 'I have a new defence tactic, no way can you win.'

Vinoo felt the tension slide off his shoulders. A game of chess with his friend was exactly what he needed. He almost always lost, but that didn't bother him in the least. The camaraderie between them when they sat at the board was eminently dearer to him than winning.

His few victories were invariably due to stupid mistakes on Vijay's side. About once in every ten games, Vijay would lose a queen or a rook making it possible for Vinoo to win. The chess set Vijay produced was his most prized possession. The pieces were carved of the finest ivory and the board was simple, but had beautifully chiselled edges. He placed the set carefully on the table between them. 'This is me being generous,' he smiled, 'you may play white.'

They did not stop at a single game. Vinoo was convinced this time that he'd win one game on merit and not by luck—unique in their chess history. Vijay embraced him across the table knocking all his beloved pieces to the floor. Vinoo laughed a little as his friend crouched on hands and knees, scrambling to pick up the pieces.

'Final Coke?' he asked, 'One for the road?' He knew his friend's addiction to the brown fizzy drink. He drank multiple cans per day, condoned by the management of the team, but definitely frowned upon. After all, he was not the poster boy for the team.

By 11 p.m., Vinoo was back in his room. He was not looking forward to the call he had to make. Aasia insisted he called her every day. 'We'll grow apart otherwise,' she had said when they were saying goodbye to each other. Her sinister smile had made it very clear he had to call her, no matter what. Fortunately, she was in one of her better moods today. 'How's my darling?' she asked flatteringly, 'Scored many runs?' Vinoo knew how insincere the question was.

Aasia knew virtually nothing about cricket. India's national passion made no difference to her. Certainly, if he played an important match she would attend, but then, she would spend hours looking bored and constantly fidget with her iPhone. As tens of thousands around her enthusiastically cheered for their team, she remained utterly indifferent. 'We haven't started yet,' he heard himself say, 'not until a few days.' As the conversation rapidly ran dry, he inquired about her new role in *Mumbai Wedding*, a sickly sweet film whose opening he would politely attend as he had all the others.

'He's so handsome,' Aasia gushed when the topic of her leading man, Farhan Khan, came up, 'not as handsome as you of course, but who is!' She laughed in a way that was undoubtedly meant to be seductive, but it drove a shiver down Vinoo's spine. 'And he's so tall, more than six feet,' Aasia continued. 'He literally towers over me. I have to strain my neck to kiss him. His relationship has just ended, poor man, he's suffering terribly.'

Vinoo was desperate to end the conversation. Deepika was waiting.

35

Dick

Dick was definitely a morning person. He used to love sleeping in, but years of broken nights—courtesy of Ben, Harry and Owen—had made him a light sleeper who was used to jumping out of bed at the crack of dawn. So when he looked at his watch and saw it was half past ten, he was stunned. When he switched on his phone, he saw two missed calls and two voicemails—Rupert Thorpe raving about his James Hawkins interview: 'That's exactly what I'd expected from you', and Julie tearfully announcing the good news; the lump was benign.

Dick could kick himself for missing that call and immediately tapped Julie's name. The tears had dried, but the emotions were still rampant. 'I've been frantic,' she said, 'a bundle of nerves. Of course I've tried to hide it from the boys, but I've been on the verge of going stark raving mad. I just wanted to scream. I pictured myself with one breast, slowly withering away into an emaciated wreck. It was so bad I'd even decided the music for my cremation.' For the first time, Julie sounded light-hearted.

'As long as it's not "Candle In The Wind",' Dick said, glad that the conversation was going in the right direction.

Julie smothered a laugh. 'Not that creep with his weird hair,' she said, 'that would make me turn in my grave!'

They chit-chatted a bit and ended the call on a loving note. Dick lay on the bed, hands behind his head, and tried to think about absolutely nothing. Half an hour later, he got up for breakfast.

It seemed as if Julie's good news had made his already hearty appetite ferocious. Bewildered, guests stared at him as he loaded his plate with sausages, baked beans, fried eggs and black pudding. The black pudding made him particularly happy. Joe and he had often had contests, betting who could eat most of their mother's home-made delicacy. He used to watch her mix the mash of oatmeal, milk, blood, eggs and whatnot until it congealed into a solid mass. 'It's a recipe from 1756,' she had always said, with obvious pride. 'I got it from my mother who got it from hers.'

Dick finished his plate, still hungry, but he was afraid of exploding if he had one more bite. With the newspaper under his arm, he walked into the lobby and was soon engrossed in an article about the gaping hole the injured Ed Morrison had left in the English team. Allan Moorcombe was keeping quiet, but Brian Jameson and the chairman of selectors, John Selkirk, seemed to have a clear preference for Maurice Flanagan. Dick was about to put the newspaper down when his eyes fell on a column—printed in italics—which had almost escaped his attention; it was titled, 'The umpire and the no-ball', extensively commentating on the incidents in Taunton and Manchester. 'Fortunately, it'll be different in the future World Cups,' concluded the scribe, who hid ironically behind the pseudonym, Hawkeye. 'Then, of course, there will only be infallible umpires.' Dick stood up, looked at the portraits of players on the wall and headed to the exit for his morning constitutional.

In the middle of the lobby, stood a familiar figure—Michael Cookson stared at the carpet, as if looking for an answer in its swirly design. Michael did not see him and initially Dick wanted to avoid his attacker of a few days ago, but in a split second, he changed his mind and purposely slammed into Cookson's back. Michael whirled around and looked straight into the face of the man whose nose he had almost broken.

'Are you going to hit me again?' Dick demanded. 'Bring it on. I won't hurt you.' A shimmer of recognition gleamed in Michael's eyes. 'What are you waiting for?' Dick challenged, so loudly people began to stare. 'Should I get a little closer?' He brought his face up close to that of the English captain and saw unadulterated hatred.

A group of bystanders had slowly circled around them. 'You were a lot faster last time,' Dick sneered, 'out of shape, are you?' The last remark was not entirely without cause, because Michael looked far from fit. 'This is the man who has to lead us to the title,' flashed through his mind, 'God help England.'

Michael had somewhat regained himself, 'Piss off, loser,' he said, pushing his way through the group around them. 'Who are you anyway? I've never seen you before in my life.'

With a smile on his face, Dick hurried outside. He would bask in this victory for a long time.

Standing on the sidewalk outside the hotel, Dick felt immensely satisfied. He, the man who went out of his way to avoid any conflict, had stood up to the great invincible Michael Cookson—and had made him looked pathetic. He reached into his pocket to call Phil and share his triumphant story. 'Your humble servant Phil Edmunds is currently unable to answer your call, please leave a message and he will call you back as soon as possible.' Dick smiled at Phil's voicemail. 'Time for a morning walk,' he said softly to himself. '*Mens sana in corpore sano.*'

He thought of his old teacher Mr Phillips's motto and turned the corner into St. John's Wood Road. On the other side of the road, he saw Graham hastening himself to the next tour. Dick was tempted to join him for another hour or two of amusing anecdotes, but just as he was about to cross the road to buy a ticket, his mobile phone rang, 'I knew you couldn't do without me,' Phil said, 'you obviously want the pleasure of my company. Well that's good, because surprise, surprise! I'm in front of your hotel.'

36

Mohammed

THAT BINGE DRINKING WAS usually followed by a massive hangover and an acute death wish Mohammed had heard. But he had never imagined that he himself would be the victim of a fire-breathing dragon clawing his way with razor sharp talons in his brain. The vomiting had left a rancid, sour taste in his mouth. He lay, utterly exhausted, on his bed wondering how to get through the day. He was satisfied with the result of his Taunton trip. Aslam Ali had delivered nicely and Hussain was pleased. James Hawkins had been approached and could wait.

Now it was Michael Cookson's turn. It was time to cash in the chip he held. Hussain had given him Cookson's contact details so he didn't have to waste any time. Hussain had influence and contacts everywhere. Mohammed had boundless admiration for his boss and looked up to him as a father. A gaunt man with an absurdly low comb-over which did nothing to hide his balding scalp, he was not conventionally handsome, but he radiated an undeniable charisma. Mohammed had gone to hell and back for him. But only once had he done a job that had filled him with self-loathing. Killing the abducted child of a TV tycoon had gotten under his skin. For days, the bewildered look of the child had haunted him. But Hussain had spoken to him, laid a gentle hand on his shoulder and he had felt better.

Michael Cookson did not answer. Mohammed tried ten times; ten times, there was no answer. The alcohol-induced eddy in his head had finally come to a standstill—it was time for some action. He had no desire whatsoever to drive through the London traffic, so he took the only taxi waiting outside the hotel. The driver leaning against the car was all but friendly, as if asking for his services was a personal affront. He heard Mohammed's destination and with a brusque wave of his hand, he motioned Mohammed to the back of the car. The drive took forever. Every hundred yards, they came to a standstill. At home, Mohammed was used to the cacophonous, unrelenting and often needless blaring of horns so it amazed him that the English underwent the inconvenience of persistent traffic jams in an almost serene calm.

An hour later and short of seventy pounds, he walked up to the English captain's house. He had decided to go for the direct approach. So, without hesitation, he bound up the three steps leading to the front door and rang the doorbell. Deadly silence. Not only did Michael not seem to be home, neither was his girlfriend Carine Stewart, of whom Hussain had told him a thing or two. Suspecting a back entrance, he walked into the side street—he was right. Looking around to confirm that he was unobserved, he attempted to open the bolted door.

For an experienced burglar like Mohammed, it was a breeze. Mohammed was amazed by the state-of-the-art kitchen he entered. He gawked at all the machines and gadgets Michael and Carine apparently needed to prepare their undoubtedly exquisite meals. The living room was worth seeing too—modern, almost sterile and everything spic and span—except the coffee table. That was a mess—a bottle of Chivas Regal next to an ashtray with more ash spilt on the table than tapped in the tray, a few butts, none with lipstick.

'Great way to prepare for a major tournament,' Mohammed thought. 'No wonder he looks like hell.' Curiously, he searched the entire house including the basement. In the basement stairwell, his eyes fell on a shred of frayed blue silk snared on a nail. Looking closer, he also noticed a strand of bright red hair in a thick dark substance stuck to the wall. His body began to tingle. Hadn't Hussain told him Carine was a beauty with fiery red hair? He carefully plucked a few strands of hair and tore a tiny piece of the blue silk, putting both in the plastic bag he always had with him—just in case. Although he had no idea what had happened there, he was sure his souvenirs would eventually come in handy.

Back in the living room, he sat on the sofa, took his diary from his pocket and tore out an empty sheet of paper. 'Dear Michael,' he wrote. 'I think it's time we meet in person. Until recently, I'd only seen you on TV, but a few days ago, I saw you in person. I did not know you were also a boxing champion. I must say, you throw a nice punch. And luckily, I had my iPhone ready at that exact moment. The picture is very sharp. Even a professional photographer would not have been able to take a better one. And there's something else. About Carine, I would love to chit-chat about her for a while. I'll call you.'

He put the note next to the whisky bottle, walked to the back door and quickly left the house. His visit had turned out to be better than he had hoped for. Of course it would have been okay to have met Michael himself, but the goodies in his plastic bag were an unexpected bonus.

There were just too many. Mohammed absolutely did not know which restaurant to choose. Initially, he thought of Pakistani cuisine, but on second thoughts, that seemed a bit too obvious. Eventually, he settled on L'aventure, mainly because the name appealed to him.

He reserved a table for two at 8 p.m. and began reading *Blood on Snow* by Jo Nesbo—a book about a fellow assassin; it did not end well. The book was just long enough to keep him busy for an hour or two. At five, he began to get ready for his date. He shaved meticulously, trimmed his eyebrows and took a 15-minute shower alternating between hot and cold—he'd read somewhere this was good for potency. At Karachi airport, he had bought an aftershave which, he now worried, might be too strong. He dabbed it sparingly on his cheeks. Fortunately, beside his linen jacket, he'd also packed a grey cashmere blazer. It was six o'clock. Exactly sixty minutes keeping him from his date with Aneesha, those sixty minutes he felt would take forever.

He made a taxi reservation for seven o'clock, and then zapped through a few TV channels. He settled on a station airing a documentary about a murder case which seemed vaguely familiar. The female suspect, however, was too ugly to look at so he turned the TV off. Nervous of being late and tired of waiting, he left at ten to seven. Outside, it was still cold. Mohammed wondered how the English survived this weather, but before he could contemplate further, someone caught his attention.

Pig Face in the faded sweatpants. He single-mindedly stepped up to the pharmacy door, apparently on a mission for more medicine. The thought of the idiot stealing even a moment of his time with Aneesha was unbearable. In a flash, he beat Pig Face to the door and grabbed him by his neck. 'You must surely have enough stock,' he snapped, 'hopefully enough to end your miserable life.' The man stiffened, not daring to look up. 'Now get out of here,' Mohammed said. 'I don't want to see you anywhere near this place in the next four weeks. And trust me, I'll be watching.' The push he gave the man was redundant as he had taken off before that, holding up his sagging sweatpants with both hands.

Aneesha was nowhere in sight, his heart sank. Had he made a mistake? Was it all just a dream? Disappointed, he was ready to turn around and leave when he heard her voice from behind the door in the back of the shop. 'Give me a moment,' she called, 'I'm just getting ready. It's been a long day, I'm a mess. And then I have to close up, there's no evening shift tonight.'

'No worries,' he replied, 'take as long as you need.' He stood in front of a cosmetics' counter and stared with feigned interested at a display of anti-aging creams.

'Fortunately, I don't need those yet,' he heard behind him. 'At least I hope not.' Caught by surprise, Mohammed turned and looked at the most beautiful face he had ever seen. In just minutes Aneesha had metamorphosed into a goddess. She wore a black and white dress with modest but seductive heels. She had done something special with her hair and there was no headscarf. 'My parents would hate this,' she said, following his gaze, 'but I'm not religious like they are.' Mohammed felt an unpleasant pang in his stomach, but held his tongue. 'The taxi is waiting,' he said, offering her his arm. 'I have an unforgettable evening planned for you.'

'That remains to be seen,' she said with a wink and in a sensual voice that made him tingle all over.

Alongside a long curtain shielding them from the other guests, they sat down on Biedermeier chairs at a beautifully set round table. That the chairs were Biedermeier was something Aneesha mentioned, who surprisingly also knew quite a bit about interior designing. Next to her, he felt like a complete yokel—an alien in the big city of London. Their waitress arrived at the table and introduced herself as Catherine. Her crow's feet revealed her age, but in her crisp white blouse and long black skirt, she made a fresh and youthful impression. 'A glass of champagne as an aperitif perhaps?' she suggested.

Mohammed, a bit baffled, looked questioningly at Aneesha who nodded enthusiastically. There, first hurdle managed. He had not forgotten his head-on collision with whisky, but the sparkling glass Catherine placed before them looked far less menacing. 'No problems with drinking alcohol?' he asked awkwardly, but Aneesha appeared to have not heard him, engrossed as she was in the menu.

It was a perfect evening. The artichoke hearts were delightful and the mussels and scallops in saffron sauce, highly recommended by Catherine, were beyond delicious. Muhammad wisely left the wine choice to Aneesha who appeared to know what she was doing. 'Learned about wine from an old boyfriend,' she said, winking. 'But don't be jealous. He's long gone.'

'Have you had many boyfriends?' He did not know where he got the nerve to ask that and felt the blood rush to his head. Aneesha was undaunted. 'A husband and two boyfriends,' she said. 'When I was 18, my parents paraded a slew of potential husbands before me. They finally made the most unpleasant choice. When I met him I knew I would always abhor him. But he was a surgeon and filthy rich. So, I ran away after two years. And you?' Muhammad realized he had to come up with a good story quickly, inventing a cricket career followed by journalism. 'You have lovely gentle eyes,' she said when he had finished. 'I'm sure you couldn't even hurt a fly.'

After the dinner, they went to his hotel room. He woke up in the middle of the night. A ray of light peeping through the closed curtains illuminated her body as she slept peacefully. She had given him all the credit; the impression that he was the greatest and most experienced lover on earth. He was tempted to stroke her naked breast, but resisted. To wake her now would be a sin.

37

Tony

TONY WAS WORRIED. IT had not escaped his attention that Michael's wretched condition was obvious to the players and staff. He knew from his own experience how annoying an intestinal infection could be—on his last visit to India, he had fallen victim to Delhi belly and had been confined to the toilet for days. But this was England, a different story here. Michael's lame excuse did not dismiss him from his obligations to the English team. Tony seriously questioned if he was even fit enough to focus on the upcoming World Cup.

Listlessly, Tony walked across the Nursery Ground to the Indoor Cricket School. The rain splashed on his neck and he was relieved to get inside. There was not much training going on this morning. Most of the time was taken up by Allan's pep talk—which made little or no impression on the players. Tony wondered if his friend had passed his prime. The tabloids were beginning to smell blood.

As he was leaving the practice grounds at one in the afternoon, Michael caught up with him. 'I need to talk to you,' he said. 'Come see me as soon as you can. In a few days we'll be holed up in the hotel and it'll be a lot more difficult to talk.' Tony just nodded. He didn't want Michael's entire mess to rest on his shoulders. He wanted to distance himself from him as soon as possible. Michael might have looked and acted like a tough arrogant bastard, but this was an entirely different situation altogether, nothing compared to the pressures of a match. This was a matter of life and death. Like a faithful old lapdog he turned his Vauxhall to follow Michael's Jaguar. They drove through the gates of Lord's and merged into traffic just as a cloud burst.

Michael sped off losing Tony within seconds. When he reached Michael's house he saw him waiting at the door; at least his partner in crime had been polite enough to wait for him. Side-by-side, they walked up the steps to the front door. Tony noticed Michael's tremors, testifying to the fact that his alcohol consumption was getting completely out of hand. Those were the hands of a burgeoning alcoholic. His assumption was confirmed by the near-empty bottle on the coffee table. Michael collapsed on the white leather sofa and pointed Tony to a chair. 'I had a visitor this morning,' he said lighting a cigarette and inhaling deeply, 'Scotland Yard to be exact.'

Tony felt sick. 'And?' he asked as flatly as possible. 'I didn't tell you everything last night,' Michael said. 'I went to see my brother near Ely yesterday and stopped off in Cambridge. I caused an accident there.'

'And you drove off,' Tony said, struggling to keep his composure.

'I did,' Michael replied. 'That's why I had to dump the Hyundai.'

'And they saw you?' Tony asked.

'Not clearly, at least not clear enough for me to be screwed. I made up a story which is besides the point now.'

'What did you make of the Scotland Yard man?' Tony asked, becoming increasingly agitated.

'Bit of a commoner really, you know—rank and file type,' Michael said, 'not too smart, I'd say. He tries to give you the impression he's thinking deep thoughts, but I don't think much is going on up there. A bloke with a raincoat like his can't be all too bright.'

Tony did not react, Michael had been an insufferable snob for years. 'I think it is best we do not speak to each other too often,' he said after a while. 'No more than is strictly necessary.' He leaned forward to swipe a cigarette and saw a note on the table. 'You've got mail,' he said sarcastically, 'perhaps a message from Carine.' He knew his comment was misplaced, but before he had the opportunity to apologize, Michael grabbed the note and began dancing wildly with it in his hand. 'Goddammit,' he cried, 'and now this! Just what we needed! Here, read it.'

Tony read it and cringed. He knew from the moment he got involved in Michael's problems that things would end badly, and he had been right. 'It is high time we put a stop to this disaster,' he said. 'It's time for a well thought out plan. I'm going home now, I'll contact you as soon as I can.'

The engine of his Vauxhall sputtered like an obnoxious brat. Checking his rear-view mirror he saw a thick cloud of smoke explode from the exhaust. 'This is Helen's fault,' he thought aloud, hoping the car would get him home safely. Without her financial demands he would have bought a more reliable car ages ago. With a sigh, he realized he would have to buy one now. It would cost him what was left of his savings and that was worrisome.

Seated in his garden, cigarette between his fingers and an ice cold beer in his hand, he struggled to put his thoughts in order. He tried hard to put Michael's note out of his mind and concentrated on Helen instead. He clearly remembered his promise to call her back, but for the life of him, he could not remember when he was supposed to. Looking at the dead flower stems caked with decomposing mass and the pots filled with last year's rotten leaves, he was suddenly overcome by melancholy.

Of course the final period with Helen had been absolute shite, but there had also been good times, or so he liked to imagine. Forgotten now were the emotional outbursts and the pointless drama of cups and saucers flying across the room. He'd rather think of their wedding night which had held so much promise. An uncontrollable urge to share this moment with her made him grab his phone. After a last, almost desperate drag of his cigarette, he tapped her name. As if she had expected his call, she answered before he could even put out his cigarette. 'Darling!' she exclaimed with a husky voice.

Tony immediately regretted the call. 'Hello, Helen,' he said formally. 'I promised I'd call back, so here I am.'

'Oh dear,' said Helen,' I hadn't expected your call for a few days, but you couldn't wait! So my suggestion to get back together is obviously just too tempting!' Tony did not know what to say. 'I'm still considering,' he said after a few long seconds, 'that's what I wanted to tell you. I'll call you.' And he hung up. He knew he had just behaved like another Kevin Higgins, the realtor who had broken Helen's heart—a bastard to use Helen's word—but he didn't care. And he had little time to muse over his behaviour as 'Driver's Seat' broke the silence of the evening. Even before he answered it, he knew what was coming. Michael needed him.

38

Michael

MICHAEL PACED THE ROOM. The first half of the note was perfectly clear to him. The incident of a few days ago had more or less gone unnoticed and he had cautiously assumed there would be no repercussions. He had assumed wrong, but he could deal with that. His first plan, to flatly deny, would obviously not work now that there appeared to be a photograph. But maybe he could buy the photographer off, although you had to be careful with extortionists, those bastards could take you for every penny you had.

But the punching incident was the least of his problems. The reference to Carine was the more disturbing issue. And the note wasn't clear, chit-chatting about Carine could mean anything. Perhaps, the author of the note knew of her infidelities. That would be easy to ignore. Or maybe he had gotten a wind of her disappearance. Maybe he knew more. The turmoil in his head was driving him mad.

Sitting on the sofa, he looked at Julian's immense painting hanging on the wall across from him. 'Damnation'—Julian had named it; a more appropriate title was hard to imagine. Completely in the style of Kiefer, his brother had used an exorbitant amount of black and grey paint and made excessive use of clay and ash.

Because he couldn't trust himself to do it, he had a carpenter hang up the enormously heavy black and grey artwork—much to Carine's chagrin.

She had hated it, had called it monstrous and suicidal. But he had insisted, and he somehow found tranquillity in the darkness of the painting, as if it absorbed all his worries. It seemed to be working its magic again as he felt himself slowly calm down and able to think straight. Try as he may, for the life of him he could not remember who else had been present when he had thrown that unfortunate punch.

After fruitlessly wracking his brain for a while, it suddenly dawned on him to check the house for signs of breaking and entering. He found nothing, the house seemed untouched. He checked the basement, nothing there either. But next to the stairs he saw something. No sign of an intruder, but a strip of blue silk and a tuft of red hair, noticeable to anyone who may have been in the basement. 'Maybe he hasn't been here,' flashed through his mind, 'or he didn't know exactly where to look'. Like an old man, he climbed the stairs. Back in the hallway he heard the doorbell ring. His first impulse was to not open, but when the ringing persisted, he decided to take the chance and answered the door.

'I'm from Babylon at the Roof Garden,' the man at the door said. 'May I speak to Carine?'

Michael was shocked.

'Or is she not home?' the man continued.

'No, she's not,' Michael answered, grateful for the lifeline. 'To tell you the truth, I don't expect her back any time soon.'

'That's unfortunate,' the voice said, 'I hope she's not missing her things.'

'What do you mean? What things?' Michael asked as anxiety started to take over.

'She left her bag at our place,' the man said, surprised. 'Did she not mention she'd lost it?'

'Not that I remember,' Michael said, fearing an attack of St. Vitus Dance.

'I found it in our "Lost and Found", and took the liberty of checking the content. Here it is.'

Michael took the bag and moved to quickly close the door.

'And another thing,' said the man, 'we're a little worried about Carine. We miss her. I don't mean to pry, but is she alright? Everyone is asking about her. She's always the life of the party.'

'No need to worry,' Michael said, pulling himself together. 'She'll be gone for quite a while, but as soon as she's back she will undoubtedly join the party again.'

'Odd,' said the man, 'she recently told me she couldn't miss London for a day.'

'Well, nothing more fickle than a woman, eh?' Michael said, hating himself for this monumental cliché. 'She'll definitely be gone for a while. By the way, who are? What's your name?'

'Richard Linklater,' the man replied, 'the restaurant and club manager. Carine and I were very good friends. She's such an inspiring and sparkling personality—one of a kind. You're a lucky man.'

'This conversation has lasted too long', Michael thought. 'See you soon,' he said abruptly.

His Jag was his best friend. When he was upset or troubled, he'd just sit in his car and appreciate the beautiful classic interior; it calmed him down, working like a tranquillizer. And he needed a tranquilizer now, but first he had to call Tony.

'I'm on my way to see you,' he said briefly, 'something new has come up and I want to tell you in person.'

'Do not come here,' his friend replied tersely. 'Someone might be watching you. What's up? What's going on?'

Michael reported his basement find and Tony was silent for a moment. 'Let's hope it went unnoticed,' he eventually said, 'I can't imagine someone looking in your basement, but you never know. Have you cleaned it up?'

Michael felt reprimanded. 'No, not yet,' he said guiltily. 'But I'm going to do it right now.'

'You'd better,' Tony told him. 'I'm going to think of a plan. You'll take it easy?'

'Sure, I'm fine,' Michael said, 'completely in control.' But when he hung up, he felt more agitated than ever. He grabbed a wet dishcloth from the kitchen and sprinted down the basement stairs. He pried the blue silk off the nail, scraped the tuft of hair off the wall and finally scrubbed the wall clean. It left a dark smudge, but there were more of them. Behind the house he set fire to his find. The burning hair smelled awful and he was glad he had not done this in the kitchen as he had initially planned.

The casino was so crowded that it took some pushing and shoving to get a seat at the bar. With a trembling hand he reached for his double whisky and waited for the impact. Across the bar, he saw a man with a weathered face wink at him. Another regular, just like him. When he had composed himself, he went to the big hall where he took a seat at a table of five. He started cautiously but soon got reckless. Although he had stuck to only two glasses of whisky he slowly drifted off into a haze. That he kept losing did not seem to register. Losing one after another, he impetuously tried to force his luck.

He only came to his senses when he felt a hand on his shoulder. 'I think it's time you and I had a drink,' he heard. 'Take a break. I hope you don't mind me being so forward?' Turning around, Michael saw the man who had winked at him early in the evening.

'Another whisky?' The man sat next to him at the bar. 'You're pushing it a bit,' he said. 'And I'm not sure that's a good thing for a national celebrity like you. Before you know it the press will get wind of it and you'll be lampooned in every tabloid—"Michael Cookson, compulsive gambler and alcoholic".'

Michael, back in the land of the living, looked at him gratefully. This stranger had just dragged him from the gates of hell.

39

Allan

Ever since the late night call, Allan constantly looked over his shoulder. 'You're getting paranoid,' his internal voice whispered. But he couldn't help it. Someone following him at night could just as well trail him during the day. Driving his Mercedes through London he was so distracted and fixated on his rear-view mirror, he nearly caused several accidents.

At home, he was restless. Valerie, sweet and affectionate after their recent lovemaking, credited their rekindled love affair. 'I thought you no longer saw me as a woman,' she said more than once, 'and maybe you're a bit jealous of Alistair.' Allan didn't know what to think of this new character in her life. He'd run into him once as he arrived home. Allan had pictured a stereotypical gay man with exaggerated effeminate mannerisms. Instead, he encountered a Lord of the Manor type in conservative tweed. 'Maybe I completely misjudged him with my Compton Street reaction,' he thought after Alistair left, 'maybe he is some kind of macho doing my wife when I'm not around.'

One more day to go and he would take up residence in the Danubius Hotel. Soon after, his team would face their first practice match against India. It had been the luck of the draw, but he would have preferred a slightly easier opponent. India had a strong team. Especially with their big star Vinoo Ramji, a phenomenal talent, who had scored a number of centuries in twenty-over matches. He was small and lightning quick and his flexible wrists could send a ball in the most unexpected direction. And, if required, he could hit the ball extremely hard. Allan remembered a massive six which had landed on the roof of the stands at Eden Gardens. The Indian newspapers praised him to no end. Vinoo was their hero, and the hopes of more than a billion Indians rested on his shoulders.

The training went well. Allan had finally decided not to replace Ed Morrison. 'Our selection is strong enough,' he told Brian Jameson who popped by for a visit. 'What about Maurice Flanagan then?' Brian mumbled. But Allan had radiated so much confidence, Brian did not argue further with him. And Michael Cookson was not a subject of discussion either. He still didn't look like he was in great shape, but appeared to have won over his lethargy and was back to training fanatically. When his troops had marched off the practice field and they'd concluded their team meeting, Alan stepped in his car and left through the gates of Lord's.

He expected the evening would involve another dinner in some posh restaurant. 'We should celebrate our last evening together,' she had suggested, 'especially now that we've grown so close again.' He'd left it at that. On one hand, he was not looking forward to the upcoming weeks of stress, with the nation's expectations so high and the cutthroat press waiting to pounce, but on the other hand, he was glad he could get away from Valerie for a while.

As he turned into his street, his phone rang. Allan could never figure out which button on the steering wheel connected the phone, but finally found the right one. 'It's time,' said the man with the deep voice. 'The time has come to hit the nail on the head.'

'What do you want?' Allan asked, a little dazed, haphazardly parking his car at the curb. 'You know I'm not up for your dirty games.'

'I know,' the man said. 'You are a man of principles, a rare species in these corrupt times.'

'Well then,' said Allan, 'why not leave me alone? '

'There is a specific reason,' the man said, 'a reason very dear to your heart.' Allan felt the conversation going in a bad direction. 'Do you remember Barbados?' the voice continued. 'That butcher really worked you over. You looked like a gangster from the East End. A dead ringer for Reggie Kray. But to change the subject—heard from Melanie lately?'

Allan was shocked. 'Yesterday,' he said. 'She wished me luck.' He did not know why he offered that last bit of information, but it suddenly seemed relevant.

'Yesterday,' the man repeated, 'but yesterday is not today. Quite sure you haven't heard from her today, because today I have her.'

Allan's stomach turned.

'I've had her send an email to her extensive network of friends, letting them know that she suddenly decided she needed a break, an urge to get away from it all for a few weeks. I must say she was very cooperative with the knife on her throat. Seems like a sensible girl.'

'You fucking bastard,' Allan hissed. 'If you lay one finger on her, I will personally strangle you slowly.'

'Now, now,' said the voice. 'Watch your temper. If you do exactly as I ask nothing will happen to her. But if you're stubborn, well, she might have to do without a finger or an ear or maybe more. Necessity knows no law. And don't tell anyone about this. Not good for Melanie.'

Allan almost choked. The man disconnected before he could respond.

Valerie was waiting for him in the doorway. 'Important call?'

she asked, as she bade him in the house with a sweeping gesture. 'I've made a fantastic reservation for us tonight. Have you ever heard of Mitsuhiro Araki—he has two stars?'

Allan understood a response was expected. 'No,' he said curtly. 'Is that a sin?'

'Of course not,' Valerie gushed. 'Alistair is wildly enthusiastic about him. He dines at his restaurant once a fortnight and is always surprised.'

Allan felt a tremendous urge to slam her jabbering mouth shut. He cursed himself for succumbing to his weakness and making love to her after so long. 'That Alistair of yours obviously has money,' he said. 'Two stars, can we even afford that?'

'Oh silly,' she said endearingly, 'you remember Aunt Anna? You haven't forgotten about her have you?' But he had. Completed erased from his memory; his wife had received a large inheritance from a maiden aunt to whom she had never paid the least bit of attention. 'I'm going to lie down,' he said. 'It's been an exhausting day.'

Valerie's voice jolted him from a deep, clammy dream in which Melanie had played a key role although he couldn't quite remember exactly how or what. 'Time for your red linen jacket,' she said. 'I want you to look fantastic tonight, I want to flaunt my man! Look,' she said, with a coquettish pirouette to show off her new gown.

'Very nice,' he said dutifully. 'I wonder how much it set me back.'

'Don't be so stingy,' Valerie retorted, 'Alistair says money should roll and I think he's right.'

Allan wished he was dead. 'I'll be right with you,' he said, 'give me a few minutes.' In the bathroom, he shaved and took a cold shower, but instead of feeling refreshed, he felt worse. He knew very well that he couldn't keep Valerie in the dark about their daughter, but he couldn't tell her now. Dreading the evening, he walked down the stairs. 'The taxi has been waiting for a while,' Valerie crowed. 'You look wonderful! I'm sure we'll have a wonderful time!'

In The Araki, they sat cramped at a long bar. Allan constantly bumped his elbow against his neighbour's. After a particularly hard bump, he turned to his neighbour to apologize.

'Never mind,' the man with the boxer's nose said. 'Oh, and by the way, thanks for the autograph you gave me at the Palomar. It was missing in my collection. And of course, good luck against India. It'll be a tough one.' Allan muttered a word of thanks and returned his attention to his 'utterly fresh, utterly perfect tuna'.

'I really should call Melanie tomorrow,' he heard Valerie. 'I wonder how she is.'

40

Vinoo

Vinoo thought of six and missed him. They had been inseparable for years. He had pet the yellow and black spotted stray wandering near his house a few times. Before he knew it, his new friend would not leave his side. It was not long before he had taught him to fetch the balls he batted far across the field. Once he sunk his teeth so enthusiastically into a tennis ball that when he returned it, it was more a sieve than a ball! But that had not affected the love he felt for his dog. And even more than being his personal ball-fetcher, Six was his confidant.

Whenever Vinoo was troubled he would sit, facing his friend, and tell him his problems. Just the look in Six's brown eyes promised him that whatever seemingly insurmountable troubles he had, it was never as bad as it looked. And he certainly had troubles now. The nagging pain in his calf which the physiotherapy could not seem to fix was the least of his problems. Of course he knew that the cricket-loving India relied on him and an injury would simply not be tolerated, but it was Dattu's threat that troubled him the most.

His conversation with Deepika had once again convinced him that she was the love of his life. Her words mesmerized him, drew him under her spell. She had none of Aasia's irksome, deceptive fakery. Deepika, in all her simplicity was virtuous, almost angelic. And now his bond felt dirty. The idea that that fat slob Dattu had ogled pictures of Deepika and him made him sick. Deep in his heart he knew he could not fix this problem by himself.

Vijay's eyes seemed to jump out of their sockets. 'I would never have guessed!' he exclaimed, 'I always thought you were a dream couple. You seemed perfectly happy to me.'

'That was all show,' Vinoo said, 'for the tabloids. I never should have married her. But what's done is done. What do you think I should do?'

'My first suggestion is to break it off,' Vijay said, 'but if I understand you correctly, that's not an option.'

'If you mean break it off with Deepika, you're right, not an option. She is the love of my life. I will not leave her.'

Vijay pressed his hands to his eyes as if he wanted to push them back into their sockets. 'Who actually is this Dattu character?' he asked, 'How do you know him?'

'Oh, I gave him a harmless scoop now and again,' Vinoo replied. 'I thought I could trust him.'

'I know you can't judge a book by its cover,' Vijay said, 'but this guy with his fat belly and unkempt beard looks pretty seedy to me—and that is an understatement. Not the type I'd expect you to consort with.'

'I always found him somewhat endearing, until now, of course.'

'That camera bit, it could be a bluff,' Vijay said, 'or did you really always stay in the same room?'

Vinoo blushed. 'We did,' he said, 'the first time we made love there it was so good that I took it as an omen. I'm quite superstitious.'

'That's too bad,' Vijay said. 'But still, he could have made it up. You can't just install a camera in a hotel room. I think the staff would have noticed. Then again, we can't be sure. Anyway, is that idiot staying in this hotel?'

'I'm almost sure of it,' Vinoo said. 'Wherever we are, he's never far behind.'

'Then I guess I'll have to talk to him,' Vijay said, with the aura of a gladiator about to face death. 'A sturdy one-on-one might change his mind.'

Vinoo looked at his friend, his slight stature hardly menacing, and laughed a little.

'No time like the present,' Vijay said. 'It's time someone taught him a lesson. He stood up and hugged Vinoo. 'Everything will be fine,' he said, 'just leave it to me.'

Vinoo, in urgent need of fresh air, took the back entrance of the hotel, pulled his hoody over his head and went outside. It was the quintessential English weather. The drizzle pricked his eyes and the wind was bitterly cold. London, in the end of May, took some getting used to after the stifling heat of Mumbai, where they'd had their last training in 98 degrees and virtually no shade in Wankhede Stadium. That was the first time he had felt a slight discomfort in his calf. It hadn't been anything drastic, and if it wasn't for the World Cup he probably wouldn't have paid it any heed, but it worried him now. While walking, he instinctively touched the sore spot. Could it be his imagination? Had he, now that he really had to perform, suddenly turned into a hypochondriac? His grandfather would have laughed.

As the drizzle turned into a steady downpour, he thought of his grandfather's house. He could picture it clearly in his mind— the long ditch alongside which there were electricity cables tied randomly together with a flimsy-looking rope, the signboard in the garbage with the appropriate text 'Help us clean our village' and the perpetual construction carried out by older women who seemed to aimlessly lug baskets of stones from one side of the road to the other.

Everything was equally dear to him. Reminiscing absent-mindedly, Vinoo found himself in an unfamiliar area. He hailed a taxi and drove back to Park Lane. He briefly stood outside the immense hotel and looked at the arched façade before he went inside. Vijay was waiting for him outside his room, he seemed extremely distressed. 'Something bad has happened,' he said in a shaky voice, revealing his agitation. 'Quickly, come in.'

'I didn't want to waste any time so I went down to the lounge immediately. To me, he seemed the type to be continuously in search of prey. And I was right.' Vijay wiped the sweat from his forehead and got a glass of water from the bathroom. 'I immediately confronted him,' he went on. 'He seemed a bit nervous in the crowd so he asked me up to his room. And that's where it happened.' Vijay drank the water as if his life depended on it.

'What?' Vinoo asked, 'What are you talking about?'

'He started convulsing,' said Vijay. 'At least I think that was what was happening, it could have been a heart attack. He grabbed his chest, began sweating like a pig, turned white as a sheet and started gagging. I didn't even get a chance to talk to him.'

'Is he still there?' Vinoo asked. 'Did you leave him there like that?'

'What else could I do?' Vijay replied nervously.

'You should have called for a doctor of course, you idiot.' Vinoo was shocked at his own words. 'Dattu is a human being. What's his room number?'

Vijay looked at the plastic strip in his hand. '407,' he said.

Vinoo thought for a split second, 'We're going to check on him,' he said. 'I do not have a good feeling about this.'

Carefully checking the hallway, Vinoo opened the door and

slipped inside, Vijay beside him. Dattu lay motionless on the bed, his obscene hairy belly on display. He was in a bad state, that was immediately clear to Vinoo. The man who had made his life so miserable was hardly breathing. In his struggle to live, he clung to a small silver object clutched in his right hand. Vinoo leaned closer and recognised a USB stick between his fingers. 'Give me a hand,' he said to Vijay, 'I think we have something very important here.'

Together they pried opened Dattu's fist—an operation requiring substantial effort. Vinoo slipped the stick into his pocket and looked around the room. 'You get the laptop,' he said to Vijay, pointing to an expensive device on the desk next to the TV. As his friend followed his instruction, he wrapped a handkerchief around the handset of the phone on the bedside table and called the front desk. 'This is room 407,' he said with a pinched voice, 'I urgently need a doctor.' After placing the key-strip in its designated slot, they left the room. It was still quiet in the hallway. Close to the elevator, they ran into a well-dressed Englishman who politely greeted them.

41

Dick

PHIL HAD RESTRAINED HIMSELF this time. No corn-yellow suit and screaming bright bow tie, but humdrum grey trousers and a snug dark blue polo neck complimenting his chubbiness. 'You'll never guess what just happened,' he said, hugging Dick so enthusiastically he sheepishly glanced around to see if anyone was looking. 'That journalist interrogated the shit out of me.' The crude expression sounded a bit odd coming from Phil's mouth, but he didn't have much time to ponder about it as his friend continued, 'You made quite an impression. If they could find you, they'd be all over you. But I hear you disappeared in a flash. Of course, the description they gave was enough for me. How many blonde curly-heads with a harelip are there? You seem to have showed that arrogant bastard a thing or two. Bravo! I always knew you had it in you; as Dorothy Parker would say, "I'm proud of you".'

He threw an arm around Dick and together they walked into the lobby. 'I couldn't get a room here,' he said after sitting down on a couch, 'but don't worry. I'm not far from you at the Carlton. I will deny myself nothing! Since Vivian has entered my life, I'm more and more inclined to take it easy. She encourages me to enjoy all the good things in life.' He winked at Dick making it crystal clear what he meant. 'And how's the writing going?'

'Excellent,' Dick replied. 'I just had an interview with James Hawkins—you know who. I got off to a bit of a rough start; writing at night and virtually the entire next day, but luckily, Rupert was very pleased.'

'What was the main topic?' Phil asked, 'Is there a theme?'

'Of course a lot about his career,' Dick said. 'But we kept reverting to the subject of the no-ball and the curious recent calls. In a separate column, I launched the idea for an electronic umpire—to register a no-ball electronically by a horn or siren. But that's not all, I also suggested a boundary that lights up and precise radiographic measuring of a four or six and a few other revolutionary innovations.

'Since it was published my phone has not stopped ringing. *The Times* and *The Guardian* called. They found it an interesting piece; *The Guardian* even hinted at wanting me to write a column for them. And there is an ambassadorship in the offing. For the ICC, no less. It is a thorn in their side that the English lotteries are getting a stronger hold on the sport—and of course all the negative consequences that are part and parcel of betting. So they're in contact with a lottery organization that distinguishes itself from the rest by giving half of the stakes to charity. This People's Postal Code Lottery is apparently quite a big success in the Netherlands and Sweden and they've developed a special format for the ICC. Are you still with me?'

Dick was afraid that Phil may have fallen asleep during his rambling. But he hadn't. 'I'm all ears,' his friend said. 'Please continue.'

'The condition is that the person, sitting in one of the six boxes in the stands reserved for charities catches the ball hit for a six, wins one thousand pounds for that charity. Provided the catcher has have bought a lottery ticket. But that will not be a problem. Who does not want their ten seconds of fame?'

Just as Dick was starting to get fired up, he was distracted by the Pakistani who had overindulged himself with whisky the other night. He was in the company of a dark-haired beauty whom he held so firmly that it seemed as if her fragile frame would break. She was dressed in a black shirt-dress and wore a headscarf loosely around her neck. Dick looked at them while his friend switched the topic of their conversation and loudly praised the many virtues of his girlfriend Vivian.

'I could not bear an airhead,' he heard, 'she has an intense spiritual life really. You may not see that on the outside, but it's true.' After disappearing for a moment, the Pakistani returned to the hall, only this time he was alone. He hesitantly looked around as if he did not know exactly where he was and then turned towards the lounge.

Dick saw his chance, 'I heard from James Hawkins yesterday that you had contacted him,' he said leaping up, 'I would be very interested to exchange ideas about the World Cup with a Pakistani colleague. I'm from *The Northern Chronicle*, by the way. May I ask what newspaper you write for?'

The Pakistani looked at him, astonished. 'I'm not a journalist,' he said, 'I'm just a fan.' He turned around and left abruptly.

'Well, I got that all wrong,' Dick said to Phil, 'but nothing ventured, nothing gained.'

'I certainly hope you don't use clichés like that in your articles,' said Phil laughing. 'Come on, let's go for lunch. The Lord's Tavern has a good reputation. Just our thing. Keeps us in the cricket mood.'

It was not busy so they were free to pick any table they wanted. 'Let's get something healthy,' Phil said, patting his stomach.

'What about a Caesar Salad?' Dick, whose stomach was not up for anything heavy at this early hour, nodded in agreement.

'Tell me exactly what happened this morning,' said Phil. 'Your performance must have been quite heroic.'

'I'd hardly call it heroic,' Dick said. 'I just acted on an impulse, no more.

'Oh, I won't accept that,' said Phil, 'come on, give me the details.'

After Dick had finished his story, Phil looked pensive. 'You can still press charges,' he said, 'what's stopping you?'

'I got my revenge,' said Dick, 'that's enough for me.'

At that moment, Graham sat down at the table next to them. He recognized them, friendlier than necessary. Dick gave him a thumbs up—a belated compliment for the tour—and received a wide grin in return. 'Shall we ask him to join us?' he asked.

'No objection,' said Phil, 'seems like a nice bloke.'

Graham appeared sincerely delighted with the invitation and joined them. He, like Dick, turned out to be an avid book collector, and that forged an immediate connection. He was the proud owner of a few nineteenth-century collectables whose titles made Dick's mouth water.

A man who claimed to possess a mint copy of the *Rules of the Old Westminster Cricket Club* from 1828 and more of that calibre was someone to look up to. Graham turned out to be a first-class conversationalist who did not shy away from gossip.

'I'm not so sure,' he said as the third mug of beer was served, 'everyone is so convinced England will make it, but what about the fact that Ed Morrison is out?'

'A catastrophe,' said Dick, 'you can't just simply replace him.'

'Indeed,' said Graham, 'and then Michael Cookson. He looks like death. I don't think he sleeps more than three hours a night. I heard from a friend who knows his way around London's nightlife that he's in the casino almost every night, with a glass of whisky in hand.'

Dick was listening intently.

This would be the sweetest revenge—an article about the

debauchery of the man who almost broke his nose. Rupert would love it. 'Can you tell me more about him?' he asked.

'That's exactly what a Pakistani recently asked me as well,' said Graham. 'That one was too curious for his own good. But I sent him off none the wiser.'

Dick ignored the slur and looked at Graham expectantly. 'I think something's up with that horrid girlfriend of his,' he said. 'How those two treat each other! My friend told me she has a rather broad-minded understanding of fidelity. So does he, by the way. Pot calling kettle black and all. I haven't seen her at Lord's for quite a while, and apparently, she's been AWOL from the social scene these last few days, in particular from Babylon at the Roof Garden where she's usually the life of the party. They're a little worried about her. They say she's left him and he's more shocked than you'd expect.'

Phil's first contribution to the conversation came as a bit of a surprise. 'I have profound insights into the woman's soul,' he stated and continued with an apologetic smile, 'trial and error, you know.'

'You and your clichés,' Dick said, laying his hand on his friend's arm. 'Can you put me in contact with your friend?' he asked. 'He may have some interesting information.'

After exchanging calling cards and finishing their fourth mug of beer, they said their goodbyes.

'I have the afternoon off today,' said Graham. 'Time for the wife and child.'

With a gallant wave, he disappeared between the cars parked on St. John's Wood Road. 'You, look rather pleased,' said Phil, 'like a happy purring cat.'

42

Mohammed

Mohammed was confused. The man who Michael Cookson had maltreated, the man who he had seen sitting in the lounge with James Hawkins, *that* man had approached him. Fellow journalist? Was that the impression he gave? He, murderer by profession, the man known as the 'Silent Killer' in Karachi's underworld, apparently had a more intellectual look than he thought.

At the bar, a lot wiser since his recent experience with the devil alcohol, he ordered a tonic and looked at the picture of Sunil Gavaskar, his father's hero. His father always said, 'He has a velvet bat. What a player!' The thought of his father took him back to the training sessions behind their house and the wonderful stories his father told him about the great players of yesteryear. He would have loved to introduce Aneesha to him. But Mohammed knew he was not here for romance, he was here for business. 'If necessary, you take up your old job,' Javed said. 'Millions are at stake. If an example needs to be set, so be it. They need to know they're not dealing with a bunch of wimps.'

'I can't tonight.' Aneesha's words stung him. If she was truly in love with him, as he was with her, surely she could make time? But she insisted she had to see her parents.

'Once a week, it's not too much to ask?'

'Yes,' he wanted to shout, 'It's too much too much. Skip this week.'

But her determined expression prevented him from pressuring her. Underneath Aneesha's sweet and soft exterior, she clearly had a solid resolve. 'I can make it tomorrow,' she said, 'I want to see you again.' It was a small patch on his wound. He took a final sip of his tonic and made his way to his room. A catnap would do him good after these last few emotional days.

It was quiet in the lobby. The blonde curly-haired man and his friend were nowhere in sight. The only audible sound came from the man behind the reception desk, who had given him his Wi-Fi code. 'Hello Mr Ahmed,' he greeted him cheerfully. 'Mr Ahmed'— he would never get used to it. When he introduced himself to Aneesha, he almost tripped over his own name. 'Mohammed' was halfway out of his mouth before he corrected himself. 'You don't even know your own name,' she teased sweetly. 'You're not suffering from early dementia, are you?' His sheepish grin had saved him that time. 'Khalid Ahmed' it was and would stay. He would not make that mistake again.

Alone in the lift, he was looking forward to a few hours of sleep with Aneesha starring in his dreams. In his absent-mindedness, at first, he did not even notice the lift was taking longer than usual. Normally, he would be whisked up to his floor in seconds, but now the lift stood still. 'Please keep calm,' it suddenly boomed from the loudspeaker. 'We are experiencing a small technical problem which we will fix as soon as possible. Again, please remain calm.'

But for Mohammed, remaining calm took an enormous effort. He broke out in sweat and his entire body began trembling. Since his brother Umar, who despite his handicap was as strong as an ox, had once pinned him under a blanket, he suffered from claustrophobia.

He was about to scream something at the loudspeaker when the anonymous voice declared it would only take a few more minutes.

Mohammed squatted down and hugged his knees. He needed to compose himself, to be strong. He did not want to exit the lift sweating like a pig and trembling like a leaf. He took a deep breath, regained himself and when he left the lift on his floor, he was back to normal.

Just as he was entering his room, someone grabbed him. The arms that grabbed his throat from behind felt as if they were made of steel. Mohammed thought he would suffocate and twisted like an eel to get out of the hold. 'You're sweating like a pig,' said a voice, 'get nervous easily, do you? Think this is bad? Just wait.' A knee in his back kicked Mohammed towards his bed, on which he landed face down. 'Do not turn around,' said the voice, 'that would be detrimental to your health.'

Mohammed's face was squashed in the pillow making it difficult to breath. 'It's time for you to pay,' said the voice, 'how many people have you killed? About fifteen is what I hear. At least that's the figure rumoured in Karachi. But some say thirty or forty.' In the silence that followed, Muhammad's brain raced. Could someone have come to London especially to make him pay for the crimes he committed in Pakistan?

The knife jabbing his backbone brought him back to the present. 'But I must be confusing you,' he heard behind him, 'don't worry, I don't care if you have a hundred murders on your conscience. I can appreciate a professional. You never get caught. The "Silent Killer", they call you. But I'm pretty good too. When I leave this room, no one will ever guess I was here.' The voice chuckled, he was apparently quite pleased with himself. The knife poking his back started to hurt. 'Javed Hussain will be a little disappointed in you,' said the voice. 'A pro like you, so easily caught off guard.

Or has the lovely Aneesha got your head in the clouds? I have to say—a damn good-looking girl. I think she's crazy about you too. And you've only just met, too bad you'll have to miss her so soon.'

The knife was now so close to a nerve end that the pain was almost unbearable. 'My boss has decided you must go,' said the voice. 'He doesn't like strangers on his turf, certainly not untrustworthy scums like you. We'll send Javed an obituary. That seems to be the polite thing to do. He'll get the message.' Suddenly, Mohammed felt the arm around his neck tightening. 'A good strangulation can take as long as you want. Loosening up now and again keeps the victim alert, keeps him in the game. And don't think you can wiggle out of this. An Indian wrestling champion cannot be tricked.' The voice was now decidedly complacent. Mohammed was on the verge of losing consciousness.

If his strangler had not allowed him a breath now and again he would have sailed off into the light. In a flash, he thought of his father; the man who had taught him the googly and so much more. And the man of the knife. The thought gave him the strength he needed to bring his hand to his pocket. 'Hey,' said the voice, 'are we resisting now?' Those were his last words. With all the power left in him, Muhammad spun around and stabbed him. He didn't get a chance to see the result of his desperate attempt as he fell into deep black darkness.

The first thing he saw was Aneesha. With a bright halo above her, she stood before him and smiled at him kindly. The vision did not last long. A nagging pain in his gullet brought him back to reality. It felt as if someone had sandpapered his throat. Mohammed sat on the edge of the bed. Slowly it dawned on him that it was a miracle he was still alive. If his attacker had applied just a bit more pressure he would have been dead. He suddenly saw the knife clutched in his hand. It took considerable effort to loosen his grip and release the knife. It was sticky with blood. And there was blood on the carpet. Not much, but still. The blood trail led to the door where it ended near the man's heart. His face had a strange grin as if he had to laugh at something nolens volens.

Mohammed realized he needed to act fast. He grabbed his suitcase, stepped over the man and left the room. He told the man at the reception he had to check out earlier due to sudden unfortunate family circumstances. 'Sorry to hear that Mr Ahmed,' he said sympathetically. Mohammed thanked him, walked to the exit where Hirohito nodded and tipped his hat.

Half an hour later, Mohammed returned his Peugeot and hired a Mini at another company. 'I hope you enjoy it, Mr Hasan,' said the clerk who accompanied him to his car. 'I'll see you when you've had enough of England.' 'Mr Hasan'—it would take getting used to. Waqar Hasan, his second alias. He hoped that he would not need a third. Mohammed knew that his role as a match-fixer would have to be behind the scenes now. Javed Hussain would have to call in help. He needed to avoid London for the next few weeks. He steered his Mini out of the city, constant traffic jams hampering his progress. At about 4 o'clock, he reached Rye, a picturesque village on the south-east coast which immediately appealed to him.

He checked in at The Rye Lodge, went to his room and called Javed.

43

Tony

HOW COULD HE HAVE missed it? Tony was sure he remembered every second of that gruelling climb up the basement stairs, lugging Carine's stiffened body. But for the life of him he could not remember bumping the wall. He feverishly lit a cigarette, hoping to clear his head. He hadn't stuck to one pack and wondered—after thirty cigarettes or more—if he had turned into an addict again. He inhaled so deeply he feared all the smoke would disappear for good. Exhaling, he produced just the tiniest wisp of smoke. Alarmed, he quickly extinguished the cigarette. This filthy habit had to stop. He sniffed his fingers and was disgusted. He scrubbed his hands in the kitchen, and then sat in his garden to think.

A strip of blue silk and a tuft of hair; that was troubling. Of course they should have thoroughly inspected the basement after hauling her up the stairs, but in all honestly, it had never occurred to him. Had the intruder seen them? Hadn't the person just come to leave the note? It could have just been dropped in the mail box. Regardless, whoever it was knew something. It was possible that he or she had indeed taken a picture of the incident, but it could also be a bluff. And Carine. Talking about Carine could mean anything.

Perhaps someone knew about her disappearance? Hadn't

Michael mentioned a nightclub where she was a regular? And then there was Michael himself. Although he had behaved reasonably the past few days, he was becoming a liability. True, he had shaved today and put on clean clothes, but his otherwise handsome face was gaunt and had a greyish pallor, unbefitting of the English team's captain—the situation was clearly taking its toll. Maintaining two alibis while the world looked on suspiciously.

Tony started to feel uneasy. 'If Michael breaks, he'll drag me down with him.' How often had that thought crossed his mind? The Scotland Yard D.I. may not have made a favourable impression on Michael, but it could very well be that behind the clownish Columbo-like façade hid a very sharp mind. Michael was not a hard nut to crack, not even for a clown. 'Stick to your guns,' he'd advised him.

'Even if your story seems unlikely, remain firm and insistent— this is what happened, nothing else.' Tony was acutely aware that the 'thinking' he had promised Michael hadn't yielded much, but it would have to do for now. He looked at the depressing dead stalks in the flower pots and resolved to clean up the mess and get fresh new flowers and plants as soon as he was home from the Danubius.

Tony never tired of watching old recorded episodes of *A Question of Sport*. Just watching the look on the mischievous mug of his old bowling hero, team captain Phil Tufnell, gave him immense pleasure. So the shrill buzz of the doorbell came as an unpleasant interruption. Clumsily, he stood up, caught sight of his Johnny Rotten-like reflection in the mirror and quickly combed his fingers through his hair.

'I thought it best I come in person,' Helen said, determinedly crossing the threshold. 'Our last call did not sit well with me. My! What a mess in here, definitely time for a woman's touch.' She walked into the room and flopped on the couch. 'This may sound a bit harsh,' she went on, 'but you've always been an indecisive dick. Important decisions were always left up to me, I constantly had to clean up after you.'

'That's highly exaggerated, and you know it,' Tony said, recovering from the initial shock. He lit a cigarette and took a long drag. 'A firm stand is required' flashed through his mind.

'The Labrador thing was just a joke,' said Helen, as she sank deep in the sofa, her legs spread indecently. 'I know you hate dogs. I can concede that.'

'So how is Kevin?' Tony said, convinced it was time to make a point. 'Still in touch with him?'

Helen looked as if she had bit into Spanish pepper, turning all shades of red.

'Have I not told you enough about that jerk?' she cried, 'That bastard cheated on me. Here, look.'

She lifted her sweater, exposing a pale breast with a purple bruise next to her nipple. 'That's his cigarette,' she shouted, 'he said he wanted to give me a souvenir. Well, he did.' Tony was reminded of Pam, his first girlfriend who had lifted her shirt in a similar way, and felt uncomfortable.

'Cover yourself,' he said, 'I believe you without all the theatrics.'

Incensed, Helen pulled down her sweater. 'There was a time you couldn't get enough of me,' she said, 'remember how you would suck my nipples for the longest time?'

She seemed to have calmed down a bit. 'May I bum a cigarette? You know I don't really smoke, but I could use one now.' She picked up a Benson & Hedges and Tony lit it. He considered himself to be a real smoker—the kind who inhaled deeply, held the smoke and then exhaled—but Helen clearly did not belong to that category. She puffed awkwardly and discarded it after a few drags. 'You don't want to be with me,' she said sadly. 'You gave me false hope. But

I forgive you.' She suddenly looked old and haggard.

'It is what it is,' Tony said relieved. He felt sorry for her as she heaved herself awkwardly off the sofa and he walked her to the door. 'Take care,' he managed to say, but Helen held her head high as she wobbled on her high heels down the garden path.

If Tony needed anything after Helen's visit, it was fresh air. He used to jog in the evening before bed and now seemed like a good time to reinstate the habit. He went upstairs and put on his training suit. Looking in the mirror he noticed it was high time for a shave. 'No time like the present,' he thought and grabbed his razor. He whet the blade and drew it across his cheeks and chin. The Pitralon, of course, was the finishing touch; he owed it to his father. Inwardly laughing, Tony bound down the stairs thinking of the winter he had been allowed to use the banana-scented aftershave for the first time. It was so strong that once outside in the freezing cold, he couldn't close his mouth because his skin was pulled so taut.

The street was quiet. It was chilly, but dry. It took a while before he finally found his jogging rhythm. He had clearly neglected his own physical condition for far too long. Massaging backaches and kneading stiff calves did nothing for one's stamina; that he knew all too well. Just as he was about to temper his already slow pace, he heard someone panting next to him. 'Another jogger,' was his first thought. 'Probably one of those fanatic, sinewy, show-offs in too-short shorts and a net shirt on his quick evening ten kilometre run, wants to beat his already impressive record on the half marathon.' But he was wrong. It was not a human being, it was Alfie, the Dobermann who he had not too long ago held nicely on a leash—the one who had given him a scar. Bob, the neighbour, was not far behind.

He came running and panting, heaving as he came to a stop, 'Sorry! I lost him,' he apologized, 'he suddenly yanked so hard

I had to let him go.' Tony was secretly happy for the break. 'No problem,' he said generously, 'Alfie and I have become best friends.' He pet the monster on the head and made some baby sounds to prove he knew how to deal with fierce dogs.

Alfie looked at him with mistrust and struck in a flash. It was a bloodbath. 'My hand, my hand! Goddammit, my hand!' Tony screamed. He held the injured appendage up like a trophy, completely beside himself. Neighbour Bob turned out to be a man of action in times of panic. He gave Alfie a smack, dropped him off at home and grabbed Tony by his arm. In his car on his way to the hospital, he tried to reassure the injured Tony. 'They'll know what to do at the emergency department. It happens, should be okay.'

44

Allan

'I WONDER HOW SHE IS.' Valerie's words echoed in Allan's mind. He too, wondered how his daughter was, and much more than that. Melanie had always been the apple of his eye and could do no wrong. He even tolerated her rebellious shenanigans when she hit puberty at around fifteen. Despite all her unruly behaviour, they could laugh together, uncontrollably at times. Jimmy had also been a trying adolescent, but he was inaccessible, distant and sullen—characteristics Allan couldn't deal with—so he favoured Melanie. And now she was gone. In the hands of someone who would not shy from atrocities. After their dinner at the Araki, Allan was in no mood for anything else, so he was relieved when Valerie eventually yawned sleepily.

'Why don't you go to bed?' he said as politely as possible, 'I'll stay up just a bit longer.' As she leaned over to kiss him goodnight, he caught a tempting glimpse of her décolleté, but kept himself in check. He poured himself a whisky and sat down on the sofa. He felt intensely lonely. He knew he would receive a call within twenty-four hours with instructions he would have to follow. If not, Melanie would pay. He looked intently at his phone as if willing it to ring. What would they make him do

188 Murder at Lord's

during the practice match against India?

The whisky sloshed in his stomach, collided unpleasantly with the fancy sushi and exploded into an acid attack that brought tears to his eyes. Any more of this and he'd be in just as bad a shape as Michael. He could not understand how Carine's leaving had Michael—a womanizer pur sang—so distressed. For a Don Juan like him, surely she was easily replaceable. Allan did not ponder on his captain's love life for long as the phone shattered the silence. 'She's fine,' said the voice. 'I wanted to let you know. Of course she's uncomfortable with her arms and legs tightly tied up and quite panicky in the dark. But other than that, as mentioned, she's fine. I'll call with instructions tomorrow.'

'Who was that?' Valerie's sudden appearance nearly gave Allan a heart attack. 'I couldn't sleep and wanted to give you a kiss,' she said.

'How sweet of you,' said Allan, trying to regain himself, 'really, very sweet.'

'But who was that?' Valerie insisted, 'What kind of crazy person calls you in the middle of the night? Do you have a girlfriend?'

'If I did, she'd hardly be so ostentatious,' Allan said. 'But no, it was Tony, something about a player's injury, nothing special. Just go back to bed.'

Valerie crept back upstairs as Allan went over the call in his mind. His precious daughter was bound—hands and feet—in a dark, dark place. He felt the perspiration on his neck. He was trapped.

And what if he followed the instructions? Would she still be murdered? Was she dead already? So often you heard stories about kidnappers claiming that a loved one was fine while in the meantime they had already been murdered. He felt his breast pocket and found what he was looking for—D.I Donald's visiting card. Should he call him or not? It took minutes for him to make up his mind and finally reach for his phone. On second thought, he decided it was better not to use his own phone. He fished Valerie's mobile phone from her bag next to the sofa and dialled the number.

Allan had expected the sleepy voice of someone abruptly awoken from a deep sleep, but D.I. Donald was alert, as if he had been waiting for Allan's call. 'I'm in trouble,' Alan said in a shaky voice, 'in deep trouble. I need to speak to you.'

'Of course,' the policeman replied, 'just tell me where and when.'

'It's complicated,' Allan said, 'I think I'm being watched. If you come here, they'll see you and if I leave they are sure to follow.

'You sound very anxious,' said D.I. Donald. 'It sounds to me like a matter we should discuss without delay. Do you think they are listening in on your phone? Could it be tapped?'

'I don't know,' Allan said. 'I'm calling from my wife's mobile, just in case.

'Very good,' said D.I. Donald, 'really, very good. Now tell me as briefly as you can what the problem is.'

Although his stomach was still upset, Allan poured a second whisky. He didn't know if calling D.I. Donald had been a smart move or not, but somehow the man who had made virtually no impression on him had given him hope. 'We're going to do everything we can to find her,' he said, 'and as quietly as possible. Let's keep in touch through this phone. I'll check every call that goes in and out.'

Any attempt at sleep was futile. He lay as quietly as possible next to Valerie, wanting to tell her, but resisting; it was not easy. At seven o'clock, he got up to make a light breakfast, his last at home, before, like Tony and Michael, he joined the team in the hotel. The cornflakes and cold milk was almost too much. Upstairs, he packed his bag. He told Valerie to go out and get a new phone as his was broken and he needed hers. She muttered half-asleep that it was fine.

In the taxi on his way to the Danubius Hotel, he contemplated his situation. His late-night call with D.I. Donald had reassured him a little then, but now he was overwrought again. The hotel's bespectacled porter politely tipped his tall hat and carried his suitcase in. The hotel lobby was quiet. He went to his room and fell on the bed to get an hour's sleep before the morning gathering began. In contrast to last night, he slept in minutes.

James Hawkins approached him after training. 'Maybe it's nothing,' he said, 'but it doesn't feel right. Tony is the only one I've told but he didn't seem too worried.'

'What are you talking about?' asked Allan, 'You're speaking in riddles. Come on, out with it.'

James's face went as red as a tomato, as if he had been caught doing something illegal. 'I mention it because of what I saw this afternoon,' he said, 'I saw something very strange, something particularly upsetting.'

'Start from the beginning,' Allan admonished him, 'with any luck, I'll get what you're talking about.' James told him about the Pakistani who had approached him and had even invited him for dinner.

Allan looked doubtful, 'A little too close for comfort,' he said after a while, 'a bit creepy, especially if he gave you his room number. But never mind, you mentioned something about this afternoon?'

'Yes,' James said, 'I finally got the nerve to tell him to stay far away from me when I saw policemen at his room door, and in the hallway. Obviously something was going on. One of the cleaners told me they'd found a body, but that was all he knew.'

Allan felt as if he was suffocating but remained calm in front of James. 'Well, if it's really serious, we'll read about it in the paper tomorrow,' he said, 'and, if it's your Pakistani, at least you have gotten rid of him for good.' He forced a smile and walked away.

45

Michael

THE THREE TEMAZEPAMS AND double whisky Michael had allowed himself did not help; sleep would just not come. He tossed and turned, and felt itchy everywhere. At five o'clock, he got up and stood in front of the living room window. In a few hours, he would join the team and a day and a half later, he would play the first practice match against India. He was not sure whether Allan would pick him to play or give a few of the reserve players the chance to prove themselves.

But if he played, the eyes of the nation would be on him. What if he failed miserably? If he stood at the wicket with the bloodshot eyes he had seen in the mirror for days, it would be a disaster. He resisted the temptation of another drink and a cigarette and went back to his bed. When he woke up, he realized he had only slept for a few hours. Despite the lack of a good long sleep, he felt strangely refreshed, almost happy. He felt a sense of resilience, as if nothing could happen to him. In the bathroom, it was clear that his energized mood was not reflected in his face, but at least it was something.

D.I. Donald was deep in thought; that was evident by the ravine on his forehead. 'Sorry, I am undoubtedly disturbing your preparations,' he said, 'but I have a few more questions. Perhaps we could go to your room, best to avoid prying eyes, especially with such delicate matters.' Michael was unpleasantly surprised. His happy morning mood was short-lived. After their last encounter, he hadn't thought much of D.I. Donald—just a stupid man with an undeserved inspector rank. But now, looking into the watchful eyes of the person opposite him, he was no longer so sure.

'I read in the newspapers that you were checking into the hotel today so I knew I could catch you here,' the detective said. 'Have you heard from your girlfriend?'

Michael decided to limit himself to short answers. 'No, nothing,' he said, 'no sign.'

D.I. Donald looked at him for a moment. Michael felt a thousand needles pricking his skin. 'I don't expect to ever hear from her again,' he added despite his intention, 'disappeared into the sunset.'

'Do you ever watch the TV show *Disappeared*?' asked D.I. Donald, 'Very interesting, not to say informative. I used to find it hard to believe that people just vanish, but there are indeed people who simply disappear into thin air, or build a new life somewhere without leaving a trace. By the way, we showed a picture of a Hyundai i20 on television asking the audience's help in finding a damaged one. And we have a tip.'

Michael felt himself falter. 'What tip?' he asked, feeling drained. 'It was a tip about a man at a petrol station who repaired a front bumper with a piece of rope. The woman who gave us the tip could not remember exactly what he looked like, so maybe you can help. Were you that man and if so, what were you doing between Cambridge and Ely?'

'This must be a mistake,' mumbled Michael, sounding more dead than alive. 'I haven't been there for years. And England is full of Hyundai i20. Plenty of them could be damaged.'

'That's true,' D.I. Donald said, 'so then, I guess you won't have any objection to coming in tomorrow for a confrontation. When we showed her your picture, she wasn't sure, so maybe if she sees you in person, it will clear up the misunderstanding.'

'I can't tomorrow,' said Michael gruffly. 'I probably have to play.'

'Not to worry,' said D.I. Donald. 'A match doesn't take all day. But still, I'll give you some leeway. Shall we do it day after tomorrow, say nine o'clock in the morning, at the Yard? Just ask for me.'

Michael hardly had any strength to answer, 'Fine,' he said, barely audible, 'I'll be there.'

'I forgot to tell you another important fact,' D.I. Donald said. 'The girl who was hit died last night.'

'You're playing, no matter what. I want to see what shape you're in.' Michael could see that Allan was worried. He felt his hand squeeze his shoulder. 'Heard anything from Carine?'

'That's the second one today,' he thought. 'No, nothing,' he said. 'And I don't expect to. Carine can be very rigid, she never rescinds her decisions. Once her mind is made up, it's done. But I'm over it.'

Allan sat next to Michael on the dressing room bench, 'And the Hyundai? I saw you were approached by that Scotland Yard man this morning.'

'They think they've seen it,' Michael said, 'someone tipped them off. That friend of Carine has made a complete mess of it. Whatever, it has nothing to do with me.'

'You did your best today during training,' Allan said, 'that was obvious. I hope you do the same tomorrow. That'll instantly squash all the rumours.'

'What rumours?' Michael wanted to ask but he just didn't have the strength. The training and the conversation with D.I. Donald had drained all his energy.

The match tomorrow—he didn't even want to think about it. Word had it that India planned to play with its strength, Vinoo Ramji, a player for whom he had the greatest admiration. He realized that he was born with a silver spoon in his mouth, while little Vinoo had had the toughest journey. An absolute natural talent, that's what he was. And he had the world's most beautiful wife. Michael had never seen a single Bollywood movie, but the premiere photos in the newspapers had spoken volumes.

If Michael's last night at home had been bad, his first in the Danubius was even worse. He had seen a television show once that stated that acute insomnia did not exist; he was not so sure about that anymore. The stock of temazepam he had received from his GP was running low. He had downed four but still couldn't sleep. Even Cyril Hare's detective novels, usually an infallible remedy when he was restless, weren't working now. They would only offset the horrifying emotions that were consuming him.

He desperately tried to remember exactly what had happened at the petrol station between Cambridge and Ely. He had bought a bottle of coke and black coffee, he knew that. And he had settled the bill with a woman who had a voice like a gravel mill. Whether they had looked at each other, he couldn't remember. He vaguely remembered not looking at her, feeling bad for her disability, but that could be wishful thinking. What if she had recognized him? There goes his story. D.I. Donald would make minced meat out of him. He could of course resolutely deny, but he doubted that would make any impression on the detective who was a lot smarter than he looked.

By 6 a.m., he could no longer lie in bed. He got up, shaved and showered with both hot and cold water, hoping it would energize him. It didn't. He sank in a chair in front of the TV, zapped a bit and ended up watching the super chef Anthony Bourdain consume so much food and drinks it made him nauseous.

The story was that when Bourdain travelled to the cities of the world for his show, he swallowed special pills so as to not throw up on camera. If that was true, he could use some of those pills right now as he sat and watched his teammates enjoy a copious breakfast. It disgusted him, his own self disgusted him; he was disgusted with the entire world.

46

Vinoo

No one laughed at Vinoo's dressing room ritual. In fact, his teammates gathered around him while he was busy doing it—a swipe down his pants, a kiss on his shirt and a tap on both shoes with his index finger. He remembered exactly when he did it for the first time, because afterwards he had scored 150 runs. He had performed this ritual religiously since then. After everybody sat down, he looked around the dressing room. It was rather pitiful, somewhat unworthy of Lord's. He found it hard to imagine that no one from the English team ever protested the sorry state of the facilities. But perhaps those crazy English were so stuck on tradition that any improvement was seen as sacrilege.

He looked fondly at Vijay who would be playing today. His eyes looked as if they were about to pop, a sure sign that he was very nervous. He had Vinoo to thank for being selected. 'He's better than you think,' he had told the coach. 'Give him a chance. I'm sure he'll do his best.' Looking at his friend now, he wasn't so sure. It seemed unlikely that his friend, hunched in the corner of the dressing room looking absolutely miserable, would be capable of great feats.

'Although it was only a fifty-over practice match,' Vinoo

thought, standing on the dressing room balcony. He was observing a sold-out stadium buzzing with expectations. The Barmy Army had turned up in droves. He watched the hordes of pale, bare-chested fans exposing their tattooed torsos to the weak sun. The famous English dress-up fetish was visible everywhere. He saw a group of penguins as well as six Donald Ducks enjoying huge buckets of beer; their day could not go wrong. And of course there were the usual nurses and meter maids scattered through the crowd.

It was not Vinoo's first match at Lord's. Two years ago, he'd had his English debut here. After his first day, the press was in a frenzy; they were no metaphors they could come up with to celebrate his magnificent performance. Comparisons with Sunil Gavaskar and Sachin Tendulkar galore, he was the new cricket god. This time too he was assailed by an army of photographers, all aiming for the best shot. As he sat down, he realized that he had not thought of Dattu for hours—his stalker who lay dying in a hotel room. Had the doctor made it on time? Had Dattu survived? He didn't quite know what he hoped for. It had been difficult resisting the urge to ask the front desk to call the journalist's room.

England won the toss and chose to bat. Vinoo had expected Michael Cookson to be one of the openers, but instead saw James Hawkins with Matt Fraser. They would slog from the start. According to the newspapers, young Matt Fraser had a lot of talent, but he was a relatively new name for Vinoo; Hawkins he knew from previous matches. He liked him. That someone with such limited skill, but so much love for the game could score so many runs was part of the charm of the game.

Hawkins asserted himself at the wicket and effortlessly sent the first ball for four across the boundary. His aggressive stance suggested he planned to do it again. The ball he received, a soft full toss, seemed perfect for him, but his ferocious swing of the bat barely touched the ball which whizzed towards the second slip; Vinoo's position. He felt something rip through his hands and saw the ball soar. Diving backwards he plucked the ball from the sky. Through the throng of teammates falling over him, he saw Hawkins leave the field with his head hanging.

Apparently, the next batsman had not anticipated such an early exit as it took minutes before Michael Cookson came into the field. Vinoo saw a ghost-white face and deeply sunken eyes. Cookson had clearly seen better days. Not that it affected his batting. Whatever the Indian bowlers fired at him, he treated it with utter contempt, as if he was playing against a bunch of hicks from some village team. He was fearless. As if he was defying death. His 50 came after 12 balls, 100 after 30. Matt Fraser, not some amateur, just stood there like an extra in a movie. Vinoo's world-class catch which had gotten the fans wildly cheering and standing on the benches had lost its charm now. While Cookson continued with his massacre, he felt a razor sharp stab in his calf. When the pain became unbearable, he motioned to the people on the boundary for painkillers. They helped, but only briefly.

While the audience roared for Cookson's next six, Nana Singh replaced him. Cookson's inning came to an abrupt end at 134. After a wild pirouette he ended up in his own wicket. Out, hit wicket. Leaving the field he raised his bat in a salute but kept his helmet on as if he was ashamed of his appearance. While the English matador was on his way to the dressing room, Vinoo felt an arm on his shoulder and he looked into the worried face of coach Dilawar Jilani. 'And?' he asked, 'is it any better?'

'We'll see,' Vinoo said, 'I'll just try and see what happens. I promise not to overstrain it.'

'325 is a lot', Dilawar said, 'we'll really need you.'

Vinoo picked at his food. 'What is it exactly?' Vijay asked, sitting next to him.

'Probably nothing serious,' Vinoo said. 'I should have let that ball go. It was much too ambitious for someone my age.' His teammates laughed, apparently Vinoo had regained his sense of humour. Vinoo noticed that even Vijay looked less worried so he decided to leave it at that. Maybe the pain *was* just the result of overexerting himself to catch that ball. Maybe he was okay again. 'You don't have to open,' Dilawar said, 'Chandu and Lala will.' But Chandu and Lala didn't last long. Vinoo half-heartedly went out on the field. From the increasingly loud buzz in the crowd he knew expectations were running high. Unlike his normal style, he began cautiously.

But after his first twenty sloppy runs, he was back. Although he didn't score at Cookson's speed, the runs came—and fast. So he could have kicked himself for whirling into the same reckless spin as the English captain—on his 113th, his wicket tumbled. Out, hit wicket. 'I don't think this has ever happened,' Dilawar said when Vinoo was back in the dressing room. 'I'll have to look it up. How is your calf, any pain?' But Vinoo was unapproachable. 'How could I be so stupid,' raged through his head, 'I am such an incredible fool.' The pain in his calf was back, and it was excruciating.

He swallowed a few paracetamols and went to stand next to his teammates on the balcony. His countrymen in the field were not doing badly at all; it even looked like they might have won when number nine got out on 324. Vijay turned ash grey. Now it was all up to him, he was petrified. Vinoo hugged him and kissed the top of his head. He took out a piece of Orbit chewing gum the assistant team manager, Hiralal, always made sure to give him, and offered it to his friend. 'You can do it,' he said. 'You can give us the win.'

Vijay was a decent bowler but as a batsman, he was terrified. There were still five balls to go and in the Indian dressing room, no one was convinced he would survive, let alone hit the winning runs. The first ball, he let go, the second, an impressive yorker, he slammed dead at his feet, the third almost ripped out his Adam's apple and the fourth was another right on the toe. When fast bowler Frank Miller started his run-up for the last ball of the game, it was deadly quiet. It was a short ball which a horrified Vijay blocked in front of his face. He ran for his life down the pitch and dove into the crease. It was a tie.

Vinoo looked at his friend who had given his all for India. He expected him to stand up, smile shyly and raise his fist in victory. But Vijay did not move. Dilawar was the first on the pitch and gestured wildly for a gurney. When Vijay was carried into the dressing room, the team doctor immediately started to resuscitate, but Vijay barely gave a sign of life. 'Quick, get him to a hospital,' the doctor said, folding his stethoscope. 'Maybe they can do something for him, although I wonder.'

47

Dick

GUIDE GRAHAM'S FRIEND PETE Clark, authority on London's nightlife, was macho and proud of it. The hair on his chest pushed through his T-shirt and his five o'clock shadow was imposing. 'Carine is a wild one,' he said after Dick and Phil sat next to him at the Babylon at the Roof Garden's bar. 'White women with red hair usually are.'

'Aren't you generalizing at bit?' Phil interrupted. 'I happen to know a few very tame ones myself.'

But Pete ignored Phil's remark. 'Not everyone likes her,' he went on, 'she's too outspoken and big on sweeping statements. Her eyes can spit fire. In short, you need special gloves to deal with that kitten.'

'How do you see her relationship with Michael Cookson?' Dick asked, 'Did she ever talk about him?'

'Not often,' said Pete, 'and the few times I did hear her say something, it was not negative. They each did their own thing and she seemed genuinely fond of him. Then again, she's a good actress, so who's to say?'

'And her sudden disappearance?' Phil asked, 'do you know anything about that?'

Pete frowned. 'No, not really,' he said, 'but we're worried. She was always here. Richard Linklater, Babylon's manager, tried to call on her because she'd left her bag here, but he got Michael instead. According to Richard, he was a pile of nerves, didn't know how to react or what to say. He said Carine had left town for a while. But where to is what I wonder. As far as I know, she had no family and she's addicted to London. Who knows, maybe I'm just making a mountain out of a molehill.'

He took a sip of his gin and tonic and sighed deeply. 'You guys should come here some night,' he said, 'this really is the hottest place in town.'

It went without saying that Phil would accompany him to Lord's for the practice match between England and India. They would meet up at the Grace Gate. Although he knew that Phil, like always, would arrive in the nick of time, Dick was far too early. He suddenly felt an urgent need to hear Julie's voice, so in the middle of the hordes streaming to the stadium, he called her. She seemed to be back to normal after the past few dreadful days. 'I dreamt of you last night,' she said. 'You want to know how and what?'

'Of course,' said Dick while pushing through the crowd, 'bring it on.'

He heard her tinkling laugh and his heart skipped a beat. 'You were really sexy,' Julie said, 'a real man, like George Clooney, but better. I think we made love three times. When I woke up I was all wet and sweaty. What do you think about that?'

Dick looked sheepishly around him. 'Great,' he said, 'wait till I get home.'

'Now that you're so famous you can get anyone, so I'll have to do my extra best,' Julie said. 'Soon, you'll be too big for Allesford.'

Dick felt a bit uncomfortable. In the distance he saw Phil arriving, early by his standards. 'I have to go,' he said abruptly. 'A kiss for the boys and a big kiss for you. I'll call you tonight.'

'Are you talking to your girlfriend?' Phil asked, 'You're as red as a beetroot.'

When Michael Cookson came out on the field shortly after the two openers, the excitement in the stands was tangible. The English captain was almost always a sure guarantee for something spectacular. But instead of his usual elegance, he now displayed a fierce brutality in his batting. He didn't seem to care where his balls landed. He just slogged away. The crowds went wild; whooping screams and shouts urging Michael on. The first 50 came fast, the second even faster. Only at 134 did the innings come to an abrupt end. This one would go down in history as the fastest innings ever recorded.

As Michael left the field, Dick looked at his notebook. It was empty. He nudged Phil to share his astonishment, but he seemed to be even more bewildered that Dick. 'The innings of a madman,' he said. 'The innings of a complete fool.' Nobody seemed to be interested in the rest of the match. Until Vinoo Ramji came on. With his elastic wrists, he batted the ball exactly where he wanted it. His 113 runs were beautiful to watch. That the match ended in a tie was extraordinary, just as it was extraordinary that both captains went out in the same way—hit wicket. And that wasn't all. The last Indian player injured himself so severely diving for the crease he had to be carried off the field on a gurney.

The double whisky he allowed himself in the bar went down smoothly. Hopefully Rupert would be as enthusiastic about his article as he was. There was almost too much action, but better too much than too little. From his seat he had a good view of the lobby where it was quiet at this late hour. He sat for a while, slowly getting drowsy, when he suddenly saw a familiar figure exit the lift. Michael Cookson was in a hurry.

With large steps he hastened towards the front door. On a sudden impulse he'd never understand, Dick jumped up and followed the English captain. As Michael stopped to light a cigarette, he froze against the façade of the building and only moved when Michael walked to the parking lot. He stepped into a striking Jaguar, but did not start the engine. Dick could see the English captain through the Jaguar's door window, smoking nervously. He slipped quickly to his own car and waited.

After a few minutes he saw Michael get out, walk away from his car, only to turn around, get in again, and drive off. Dick followed him at an inconspicuous distance, occasionally letting a few cars pass between them. Because Michael was driving at a normal speed, it was easy to keep him in his sight. Half an hour later, they had left London behind them. Dick had no idea where he was going. When they reached a dirt road and it was impossible to follow unnoticed, he dimmed his lights and stopped. In the distance he saw how Michael's car veered to the right of the track. He stepped out of his car and moved as quietly as possible towards the Jaguar. It stood still in a clearing with lights on and the engine running.

At least that's what Dick thought, until he saw the car move and with a sudden roar of the engine, it disappeared over an edge. He realized he was witness to a catastrophe. The ear-shattering splash that followed the disappearance of the car confirmed what he had just seen. Looking over the edge he saw how the rear of the Jaguar disappeared in the black water. He had heard of people who, in a situation like this, immediately threw their clothes off and jumped fearlessly in the water, but the black hole paralyzed him with terror.

After what felt like an eternity, he made his way back to his car, checked his satnav only to find it didn't recognize the road he was on. His impulse as a news-hungry reporter was to stay, but at the same time he realized there was nothing he could do here. At a snail's pace he drove down the dirt road until his satnav picked up his location.

Before he drove away, he called 999 and without mentioning his name, he briefly explained what had happened. At 2 a.m., he was back in his hotel. He had an almost uncontrollable need to hear Julie's voice, but decided not to disturb her. When the first morning light broke through the curtains, he fell into a restless sleep.

48

Tony

'IT HAPPENS.' THE WORDS of neighbour Bob were ringing in Tony's ears as he walked into the emergency ward with Bob at his side. His hand was a mess. With his titanic jaws, Alfie had sunk his teeth between his tendons and bones. The doctor looked worried. 'I hope nothing vital has been damaged,' he said. 'What do you do for a living?' At that moment, Tony realized the magnitude of the disaster.

His hands, his magical hands, with which he massaged injured players, would be out of business for a while. He could picture Allan's face. After the wound was stitched and he was provided with a sling, he left the hospital with Bob at his side. At home on the sofa, he lit a cigarette and just sat there, stunned by what had happened. He was almost tempted to call Helen but didn't. After a sleepless night he checked himself into Danubius. The task ahead loomed.

Allan's reaction was muted. 'It's up to you to decide who should take over the heavy work, that's not my business.' Tony immediately called his assistant Gary Jenkins who was both sympathetic and delighted at the same time. Gary was an ambitious boy, eager to boost his career and had always resented playing second fiddle. 'I'm ready,' he bellowed through the phone, 'you can count on me.' But his services were not needed during the match. None of the English players needed help which was in stark contrast to the Indian team. The tension had been too much for their last man Vijay Apte.

While he was being carried off the field, Tony looked around for Michael. He, apparently, had not waited for the blood-curdling end of the match but had retired to the dressing room. What the English captain had been thinking during his innings was a complete mystery. He had danced around the wicket like a possessed dervish. Tony had tried to make eye contact as Michael left the field after his incredible display, but the English captain looked at nothing and no one.

The news of Vijay Apte's death didn't reach Tony until late in the evening. After the group dinner, from which Michael had excused himself complaining of a mild nausea, the pain drove him to his room where he lay on the bed. He hadn't taken any of the painkillers the hospital had given him, but they were a godsend now. Working as a painkiller and a sleeping pill, it put him in a deep sleep.

The loud banging on the door woke him up. 'I thought you should know,' Allan said. 'We'll have to release a statement in the morning. That goes without saying.'

'How awful!' Tony said, hardly awake. 'Is there a cause of death?'

'I haven't heard anything yet,' said Allan, 'but I think it was a heart attack.'

'You hear that a lot,' Tony said.

'Someone can live their entire life without knowing they have a heart defect, and then suddenly, it becomes fatal. If that's the case with Vijay, the tension certainly didn't help. I have rarely seen such a hair-raising end.'

After Allan left, Tony lay down again, but sleep was out of the question. After tossing and turning for a while he acknowledged it was useless and went to the bathroom to refresh himself. He splashed a generous amount of water on his face, went back to the room and dropped into the armchair in front of the TV. At that moment, he caught sight of something white on the floor. He went to retrieve it and saw it was an envelope someone had slipped under his door. Back in his chair, he read 'For Tony' written on it—nothing else. He ripped open the envelope, almost tearing its content in his haste and read:

Dearest, dearest friend,
This will be the hardest letter of my life. From the salutation, I hope you can read how much I have appreciated your friendship and solidarity. Ever since the West Indies I knew I could count on you. You were the only person I had ever shared the Muriel story with and how deeply she hurt me. Of course, I knew you were a trusted confidant for many, but in my arrogance, I always thought I could handle whatever came my way alone. My conversations with you greatly eased my mind. But now the net is closing in around me and I feel completely alone. I assume you will not read this letter until tomorrow. You are free to share the content with D.I. Donald of Scotland Yard. You can also tell him that I killed Carine and am responsible for the death of the girl in Cambridge. That should be it. Leave Carine's and my grave rest untouched. I want eternal peace.
   If I were you I would tell what needs to be told anonymously, there is no need for you to be involved. You don't deserve any form of punishment. I, and only I, am responsible for what has happened. That I have

chosen this ultimate end has everything to do with my selfishness. When all of this comes out I will be kicked off my pedestal—and I can probably live with that. But I can't see myself locked away in prison for years. And I do not believe that I will be able to continue lying and cheating if I have to face a cross-examination. I feel like I am slowly disintegrating. Tomorrow I will disappear from the face of the earth. The English captain vanishes into thin air.

Goodbye, Tony, good friend, I hope you will miss me a little.

Michael

Tony sat staring into space for a few long minutes. There was a time when he had seen Michael as an invincible, egocentric hero; indifferent to anyone or anything.

Of course, he had seen the cracks in his shield the last few days and he had watched him starting to break—most visibly during his last innings, but he had not seen this coming. He got up and went to Michael's room. The door was ajar, as if the occupant was expecting a friend. Inside, it reeked of smoke and the four small empty whisky bottles from the refrigerator revealed that Michael had needed a bit of Dutch courage. Tony sat down on the bed, his head in his hands. When he looked up he saw the 'no smoking' sign and in spite of the horrible situation, he had to smile. Michael had never played by the rules.

Back in his room, he did not hesitate for long. The Yard's switchboard operator heard the urgency in his voice and put him through immediately. The policeman seemed unaffected at first, but a slight tremor in his voice eventually betrayed his emotion. 'That's quite a story,' he said after Tony had finished. 'But you forget one thing—the tangible evidence. In other words, where is Carine's body and where is the Hyundai?' In the silence that followed, Tony picked up Michael's letter and read what his friend had asked for. Should he respect his last wish or come clean with it all?

'Are you still there?' he heard the voice at the other end of the line ask. 'Do you have anything else to say?'

'I'll call you back,' Tony said, 'I need some time to think.'

49

Mohammed

'SILENT KILLER' MOHAMMED MUSA'S stay at The Rye Lodge was short-lived. A composite drawing of a man who had stabbed someone in the heart in the Danubius Hotel had aired on TV. The likeness was not great but good enough for Mohammed to pack his bags in haste. Near Battle, he rented a wooden bungalow from a sleepy-looking woman in a somewhat sleazy holiday park. He immediately contacted Javed Hussain who had already taken precautionary measures. 'The speedboat will pick you up tomorrow at eleven,' he said, 'make sure you're there. I'll let you know exactly where.'

Mohammed asked astonished, 'Has it all been for nothing?' 'No,' Javed said. 'It has not been for nothing. There is always a Plan B and if that doesn't work, a Plan C. Your successor is already in England. He'll take over. You need to lay low. Have as little contact with people as possible.'

Aneesha! Aneesha! In his loneliness he could think of no one else. Would he ever see her again? Would it just be that one night? He had called her the minute he had arrived in Rye to reschedule their dinner date, not knowing that Javed had other plans for him. Would he dare go against his boss's orders? He knew Javed's reputation. Mohammed had cleaned up quite a few people who had crossed Javed in one way or another. But it was impossible for him to resist the urge to call her. Her initial reaction was lukewarm at best, but eventually she gave in. 'Dress up to the nines,' Mohammed said, 'we are going to a top-class restaurant, we won't settle for less.' From her laugh he knew the ice was broken.

When she allowed him to pick her up at her home, Mohammed thought it was proof of their intimacy. It made him feel warm throughout the drive to London. His satnav, which took him five or six attempts to figure out, brought him effortlessly to her apartment. He had not expected her to be waiting for him in the doorway, but there she was, in all her beauty. She wore a lilac dress and her hair was pinned up. Mohammed was awestruck, he tried to hide his emotions but on the inside, he was aflame. This was the woman who would rule the rest of his life. This woman who he would see for the last time tonight. The woman he loved with every fibre of his being.

With great effort, he managed to give her a friendly and interested smile. 'I didn't think it was possible, but you look more beautiful than the last time I saw you,' he said. It was not the best opening line, but it would have to do, because it was all he could manage. Relying on his satnav, they drove to The Square. He had tried to reserve a table at Gordon Ramsay and Alain Ducasse—both had three stars—but they had been booked for months. So, he had to settle for a restaurant with only two stars. It was simple but very chic. Mohammed pulled out the purple-striped chair for her and Aneesha gracefully sat down.

During the nine-course 'Sample Menu'—tiny little portions fit for a mouse—Mohammed had problems trying to get anything down his throat. The 'Porthilly Rock Oysters', the 'Smoked Lincoln Eel' and the 'Roast Ernest Soulard Foie Gras'—they looked delicious, but he found them disgusting. Aneesha did not seem to notice and shared stories about her youth in Islamabad and her arrival in England. 'My father thought he could take his career as an ENT specialist further in the UK,' she said. 'In Pakistan, he was the top specialist, but in England, he had to start all over again.'

'And?' Mohammed asked as he raised his eyebrows to show his curiosity. 'Of course he succeeded,' said Aneesha. 'I have never known a more ambitious man than my father. He is the prototype of an overachiever.'

'That does not sound pleasant,' Mohammed said. 'Do you love him?'

'No,' said Aneesha, 'and however shocking it may sound, I don't really love my mother either. They are conservative. I've already told you about the man with the most insipid handshake in the world who they chose for me. The two years I was his wife were the worst of my life.'

'You're a brave woman,' Mohammed said. 'Not everyone would have had the guts to walk away. Do you have any brothers or sisters?'

'A sister,' said Aneesha,' and she wears a burka.'

As she spoke, a dark cloud passed over her face. Mohammed did not ask further. He could think of only one thing. Go. Go away with her to the ends of the earth. Go to a place where the long arm of Javed Hussain or Scotland Yard could not touch them. Visons of a tropical island with a radiant blue sky and tall swaying palm trees now held his attention more than the conversation with Aneesha. 'You're dreaming,' she said with a smile. 'Your mind has wandered off. Apparently, I'm not interesting enough.'

'You're completely wrong,' Mohammed said, feeling caught.

'Well, what did I just say?' said Aneesha, 'come on, tell me.' 'Your sister wears a burka,' Mohammed said, racking his brain, 'that was the last thing you said.'

'Then you're way behind,' Aneesha said. 'I also said that she always spied on me at home. The moment I took my headscarf off my parents knew about it, if I used make-up, even if it was just a little, they knew. Now she lives in Nottingham with a man who hits her and has had three children in three years. I have no contact with her.'

'And with your parents?' Mohammed asked.

'I see them regularly,' Aneesha replied, 'despite everything, I can't seem to do without them.'

Thanks to the excellent wine, by the time they'd reached the seventh course, Mohammed finally began to relax. He listened attentively to his beloved's humorous stories about the daily exploits at The Lord's Pharmacy. 'He was back this afternoon,' she said. Mohammed knew immediately she meant Pig Face with the drooping sweatpants.

'I hope he did not bother you,' he said. 'Do I have to teach him another lesson?'

'That's no longer necessary,' Aneesha said. 'He will not get a single pill from us anymore; he'll have to look elsewhere. That fool had the nerve to complain to my boss about your behaviour. But he listened to my version of the story and drew his conclusion.'

'That's excellent,' Mohammed said, 'you know, all you had to do was wink and I'd have come by in a flash.'

As he spoke, he realized how hollow his words were. He would not have come by at all. The speedboat would have dropped him somewhere on the northern French coast and Javed would have organized further transportation. Due to the gloom that overwhelmed him, he hardly enjoyed the dessert. Fortunately, Aneesha did not seem to notice and carried forward much of the conversation. At eleven o'clock, Mohammed realized the time for goodbyes had arrived. Javed would be mad enough about his evening out, let alone a whole night of lovemaking.

'That's quite an amount, shall I chip in?' Aneesha asked, glancing at the bill, 'That's more than I spend on food in a month.'

Mohammed shook his head, gallantly drew back her chair and offered her his arm.

The man waiting for him as he stepped out of the restaurant was especially friendly. 'Your name please,' he said, showing his identification.

'Khalid Ahmed,' Mohammed said stuttering. 'But why do you want to know?'

'Because a body has been found in your hotel room,' said the man.

'Maybe you can tell us more about that.'

Mohammed felt Aneesha untangle her arm from his.

'Don't worry about the lady,' said the man. 'We'll drop her home safely. You're coming with me.'

While he was escorted to the unmarked car parked on the curb, Mohammed did not look back. He could not bear to look at Aneesha. No one spoke in the car.

'How could I be so stupid?' The question raced a thousand times through his head. Javed had been so good to him. All he had to do was lay low until the speedboat picked him up. Not anymore. Because he, like an idiot, had to dine in a two-star restaurant while his photograph had been aired on national TV. It had been a miracle Aneesha hadn't seen it.

They found his knife at Scotland Yard immediately when they did a body search; he was not surprised. He had not gotten rid of it after he stabbed his attacker. It was his father's knife. That would have been sacrilege. 'Used it recently?' said the man who searched him further while holding the knife in front of his face. Mohammed saw a dark streak on the badly cleaned blade and realized that his story—which he had to keep Javed out of—would never be credible.

The interrogation did not last long. 'Tomorrow, we'll certainly make more time for you,' said the man who had arrested him. 'Better be prepared for a few gruelling hours.' Between two policemen, he was escorted to his cell. Afraid that he might do something to himself, they had taken everything away from him. All he had were his pants—which he had to hold up with both hands—and a T-shirt. Mohammed thought of Aneesha, remembering how she had let go of his arm. He lay down on the cot, the only piece of furniture in his cell. With his eyes shut tight, he tried to focus on his situation. But after a few minutes, he had to conclude it was hopeless. Mohammed Musa, alias Khalid Ahmed, alias Waqar Hasan, was arrested. The 'Silent Killer' was as good as dead now.

50

Allan

THE CALL CAME FIFTEEN minutes before the start of the match. 'I saw on ESPNcricinfo that England has won the toss and is going to bat,' said the man with the deep voice. 'Take precise note of what I'm going to say to you now. Instruct your first batsman to take it very easy. Tell them to carefully build up their innings. In particular, make sure Michael Cookson understands—a premature wicket loss is deadly. England cannot make more than 250 runs.' 'I'll do my best,' said Allan, who had left the dressing room and gone out into the hall, 'but I can't absolutely guarantee it.'

'Who are you kidding?' said the voice, 'Your team listens to every word you say. You know it and I know it. Oh, and Melanie is doing fine. She panics, but who wouldn't in her circumstances.'

Allan was boiling with rage, but he controlled himself. 'When do I get her back?' he said with a constrained voice.

'Now, now,' said the man, 'always in such a hurry. There are still plenty of matches to go. But if you follow my instructions, nothing will happen to her.' Walking into the dressing room, it took Allan almost superhuman effort to radiate the calm confidence of a good coach just before a match. In a short speech, he told his team what he expected of them. No one protested. Only Michael stared at him with his bloodshot eyes. Allan was tempted to take him apart, but left his captain alone—he seemed to have enough problems of his own.

After the match, Allan was frantic. 325 was not 250. The man with the deep voice would not accept this. Michael's unprecedented slogging had caused this his explosion of runs had thwarted the plan. At the end of the match, Michael just sat there, motionless on his spot in the dressing room—while rest of the players chattered excitedly about the surprising end of the match. A messenger came back from the Indian dressing room with disturbing news. Vijay Apte was in bad shape. Death on the cricket field—Allan had seen it before.

Usually it was a freak accident like the Australian Phil Hughes who had missed a hook which slammed into the back of his head, shattering his vertebral artery. When he was young, Allan had experienced an overweight Saturday afternoon cricketer paying for his obesity with a heart attack on the field. But Vijay was not fat or old and had certainly not been hit on the head—with a ball or otherwise.

On his way to get more information himself, he ran into the Indian manager, who told him gravely that Vijay was in an exceptionally bad state. Distraught, Allan informed his players. Everyone was devastated. Except Michael; he showed no emotion.

𝟅

'It must have been providence,' said D.I. Donald, whose cleft was less pronounced than usual. 'I'm sure you can tell I was brought up a Catholic. In times of need my mother always prayed to Our Lady of Perpetual Help. When it went well she would be deeply grateful and if it didn't, she never blamed Our Lady.' He wiped the perspiration of his forehead with a bandana and sighed. 'And it went well. You will see your daughter tonight.'

Allan was ecstatic but contained his excitement so as to not draw attention in the busy Danubius lobby. 'How is she? Did he do anything to her?'

'As far as we know, no,' said D.I. Donald. 'Of course, she's pretty shaken up, but after what she's been through it's not surprising. She was in mortal fear for days. Even the toughest commando would be rattled.'

'But how did you find her so soon?' Allan asked.

'A combination of luck and expertise,' said D.I. Donald. 'Our phone tap showed that the call this morning came from north of Gerrards Cross. Not quite a needle in a haystack but challenging enough. We searched the entire area for remote farms and barns, but nothing panned out until I saw it. It was just a flash in the corner of my eye. We'd almost passed it. I have to say it's all thanks to my hobby.'

'Hobby?' Allan asked bewildered. 'What has your hobby got to do with it?'

'I collect model cars,' said D.I. Donald, whose cleft was deepening now. 'Old and new. I have more than two thousand.'

He paused, allowing this astonishing fact to sink in. 'And I had just bought one. You don't see an Aston Martin DB 9 every day. A fancy car like that in a rundown shed seemed a bit suspicious. I mobilized all my men. And when we stormed the shed in the evening, we took them completely by surprise. There were three of them and your man with the deep voice was one of them. He seemed to be the boss.'

'Where is Melanie?' Allan asked. 'I want to see her as soon as possible.'

'I understand that,' said D.I. Donald. 'She's still at the Yard.

We obviously have a lot of questions to ask her. But I think she can make herself free for her father.' He laughed mischievously and walked with Allan to the exit. 'And we found more,' he said. 'Very interesting things, but unfortunately, I cannot tell you about that.'

When Allan watched a dramatic reunion in a TV series, he was often moved to tears—tough on the outside, soft on the inside. But when he was reunited with the apple of his eye, he couldn't shed a single tear, as if his all emotions had been frozen. But after a few minutes of holding Melanie so tightly in his arms she could hardly breathe, he finally burst into tears and all his locked-up emotions were released. From the Yard, he called Valerie who was horrified, firing off a fusillade of frantic questions at him. Allan was glad he could cut the call short with the announcement that they would soon be on their way home.

He didn't get much detail or background about what exactly had happened or who the people were. 'It's a big Indian syndicate,' was all that D.I. Donald was willing to reveal. 'But, as you may know, we are dealing with a Hydra—chop off one head and two return. This is just the tip of the iceberg.'

Allan didn't care. He wanted to go home. And for the time being, he didn't care about the English team either.

51

Vinoo

VIJAY WAS HIS DADDY'S boy. He often spoke of the little big man who had raised him virtually on his own. His mother was hardly ever present in his stories. Only once had Vinoo explicitly asked his friend about his mother, and he was met with a un-Vijay-like silence. And now he had to inform the little big man of his son's death. Since Vijay had been brought to the mortuary Vinoo had been in a trance. As if hypnotized, he kept seeing the dead face of his friend, wandering in his mind's eye. His hand had reached for his phone several times, only to draw back at the last moment. But he knew he had to call. He couldn't let Vijay's father learn of his son's death from the press.

The sadness spanned across thousands of miles. 'My only child, the light of my heart, I was so proud of him,' Vijay's father stammered. 'How in God's name is this possible? He has never been sick, not a day in his life.'

'The team doctor said this happens,' Vinoo said, 'he has seen it before; a player dying of a heart defect he didn't know he had. He doesn't think an autopsy is necessary.'

'I don't want anyone cutting into my son's beautiful body,' Vijay's father said. 'I want him home for the cremation.'

'He is likely to be released soon,' Vinoo said. 'I will bring him home to India.'

'But what about the matches?' The man seemed to forget his grief for a moment.

'The first official match only starts in a week. The rest of the team will stay here and hold a memorial.' Vinoo didn't know what else to say and after a few more comforting words, he hung up. He was well-aware that he had failed to console his dead friend's father.

After the quiet dinner with his teammates, Vinoo retired to his room. But by ten o'clock he could no longer bear to be there. He wanted to go to Vijay, his friend whose body lay, lonely in the morgue. Fortunately, someone answered the phone at the mortuary and after he explained the special relationship he had with the deceased, they allowed him to come. In the taxi to the mortuary, he had a sudden seizure which greatly unnerved him. It subsided after a few minutes but left him feeling weak. The man who greeted him at the mortuary door was—with his grey skin, elongated face and yellow teeth—the personification of a gravedigger, but that did not affect his sincere kindness. 'I'll leave you alone with your friend,' he said compassionately as he pulled out the morgue drawer. 'Take your time. I'm here for a while.'

Vijay certainly did not look peaceful. His face had a contorted grimace he had never had in his life; as if death had struck him an unbearably painful blow which had taken all of his strength to fight. Vinoo pulled up a chair and sat next to his dead friend. The hand he felt under the sheet that covered him was ice cold. All the life in the body had departed for far, unreachable places. As he stroked his hand, Vinoo thought of the first time he had met Vijay.

It had been many years ago but he remembered it well. The

perpetual mess of Vijay's cricket bag—the never-ending piles of smelly trousers, shirts and sweaters that spilled from his bag onto the dressing room floor—had initially irritated Vinoo, but when he had looked into the innocent bulging eyes of the boy who had later became his best friend, he had not been able to contain his laughter.

Suddenly, he felt the need to see those eyes again. He bent over the body and with both his thumbs, he gently opened Vijay's eyes. Vijay stared at him with his familiar surprised look, but their lifelessness shook Vinoo and he quickly shut his eyes again. After gazing at his friend for a while, he called the man with the gravedigger's face who closed the drawer and accompanied him to the exit. The taxi had waited for him and now brought him, in the drizzling rain, back to his hotel.

'D.I. Ferguson is the name,' said the tall pale man with Ian Rush-like moustache waiting for him in the lobby. 'I'm D.I. Donald's colleague and am assisting him in this case. Glad to catch you because it's a matter of utmost importance.' He emphasized his last words as if he wanted to make a specific point. 'Perhaps we can go to your room? Not only is this case important but it is also highly confidential.'

'Of course,' Vinoo said as he led the way to the lift. The policeman's words hardly sank in as he was still under the spell of those dead bulging eyes. Not a word was spoken in the lift. D.I. Ferguson only resumed talking when they reached Vinoo's hotel room.

'I'll get straight to the point,' he said. 'Have you been threatened lately?'

Vinoo was shocked. 'Threatened?' he repeated a little inanely. 'No, not that I know of.'

'Nothing has happened which may have given you cause to

call the police?' said the man whilst plucking at his moustache. Vinoo thought of the dying Dattu Lal and felt the same weakness he'd felt in the taxi; luckily not the shakes—that would not do in front of a policeman.

'No,' he said again, 'I have not noticed anything special.'

'We have,' said D.I. Ferguson, 'that's why I'm here. You are in great danger.'

Vinoo felt very uncomfortable now. 'What do you mean?' he asked, realizing he had to appear as naive as possible.

'I cannot tell you everything,' said the policeman, 'but the following is vital and you need to know. An Indian gambling syndicate wants to use you to set an example. You are considered incorruptible and in their eyes everybody in and around cricket must be corrupt. Massive amounts of money are at stake as you've undoubtedly heard, and incorruptible people are of no use to them. You, as Indian cricket's figurehead are the intended example that will force the rest into submission.'

Vinoo looked at the man and his moustache, or what was left of it. Dattu Lal kept popping up in his head; his failed attempt to bribe him still vivid in his mind's eye. 'They are conniving,' said D.I. Ferguson, 'and inventive. Do you often chew chewing gum?'

The sudden change of subject surprised Vinoo.

'Only during a match,' he said. 'Hiralal, our assistant manager always gives me a stick of gum before a match, it helps keep my nerves under control. It's sort of a ritual. I'm not the invincible God India makes me out to be. I too get nervous.'

'Do you ever deviate from that ritual?' D.I. Ferguson looked at him intently. The 'no, never' was already on Vinoo's lips when he remembered he had not taken a chewing gum in the practice match because he had been too preoccupied with pain and painkillers.

'This afternoon,' he said after a pause, 'this afternoon I gave it to a teammate who had to play the last over and could use it.'

D.I. Ferguson turned white. 'As a cricket lover, I know this was Vijay Apte,' he said flatly. 'And Vijay Apte is dead. And you should have died in his place.'

Vinoo almost threw up. 'What do you mean? How is this possible?' he asked.

'This afternoon we raided a shed just outside London,' continued D.I. Ferguson, 'not only did we find a few kidnappers and their victim, but also a comprehensive plan detailing the death of Vinoo Ramji on the field.'

'What's that got to do with chewing gum?' Vinoo asked bewildered.

'Are you familiar with the yellow oleander?' the policeman asked.

'Yes,' said Vinoo, a bit surprised, 'I know it very well. My grandfather used to use it in tiny doses when he had a stomach ache.'

'Good. Then let me explain,' said D.I. Ferguson, sounding like a professor. 'The yellow oleander is a small, tropical bush with, as the name implies, yellow flowers. It yields yellow fruit which ripen red and dry black.' He cleared his throat as if he were preparing for an apotheosis.

'The yellow oleander is very poisonous,' he resumed. 'This is because of the the vetin found in its seeds. A large dose can cause a fatal heart attack and that large dose, in a concentrated form, was in the chewing gum you gave to Vijay Apte before he went on the field.' He heaved—the rasping breathing was the sign of a seasoned smoker. 'I know you two were inseparable,' he continued, 'so, 'I'll leave you alone now. Of course there will be an autopsy, but the outcome is clear it seems. I assume the body can be sent to India quickly. Oh yes, and I'll speak to Hiralal now. He has a lot to explain. And I trust you can keep this conversation to yourself.' Vinoo nodded. He knew it would be difficult, but he also knew that he would keep his promise.

After D.I. Ferguson left, Vinoo wanted more than ever to hear Deepika's voice, but she did not pick up. Instead, Aasia called and, in a cheery voice, told him all about her wonderful relationship with her leading man, Farhan Khan. 'He's so handsome,' she sighed, 'and I obviously excite him.' Vinoo didn't ask how she knew that, hoping to keep the conversation as short as possible. It didn't even occur to him to tell her what had happened that afternoon. Aasia was oblivious to the fact that her Bollywood gossip did not interest him even remotely and chattered on. In the middle of a distasteful story about her director's sexual aberrations—an appalling blubbery man who Vinoo had met once and instantly disliked—he heard the tone of an incoming call. He didn't care that he had to cut Aasia off. He just wanted to switch to the new caller. It was Deepika.

'I just missed your call,' she said. 'How lovely to hear your voice, is everything going well there in faraway Britain?'

'Not really,' said Vinoo. 'I might as well just say it. Vijay died on the field this afternoon, I think it was supposed to be me.' It was quiet on the other end of the line.

'I don't understand,' said Deepika. 'What do you mean?'

'It's a long story,' he replied and began to tell her.

'So I almost lost you,' Deepika said after he was finished. 'It's actually a miracle that you're still alive.'

'An unbelievable coincidence, no more and no less,' said Vinoo, moved by the soft cry in her voice.

'The newspapers will be full of it tomorrow. As soon as the body is released, I will leave for India to attend the cremation.

The only good thing about the whole situation is that I can see you. At least, I hope so, because after the ceremony I will have to rejoin the team as soon as possible. The World Cup waits for no one.' The enormous sadness that engulfed him made further conversation impossible.

'I'm utterly worn out, completely exhausted,' he said, 'but I wonder if I'll be able to sleep at all'.

52

Dick

THIS EARLY MORNING HAD no gold in its mouth. Looking at his watch, Dick saw it was 4 a.m. The pale morning light cast vague shadows around his hotel room. He felt awful. Not because of the lack of sleep but because of what he had just seen. The death of a great athlete. Despite the fact that he had behaved so appallingly towards Dick, the scene he had witnessed had devastated him. Closing his eyes, he saw it all again—the car on the edge, the silhouette behind the wheel, the dive into the deep. Why, during his 999 call, had he not just called a spade a spade? Why the mystery? He would have liked to ask Phil for advice, but he was probably fast asleep.

The temptation to call 999 again was strong, but he delayed the decision. He sat in front of the window for a while, watching a train purposelessly chugging back and forth. It was drizzling again, as it had been the last few days—it was a wonder they had been able to finish the match yesterday. He took a bottle from the minibar and let the whisky do its job. After the second bottle he felt almost content. He picked up his phone and called 999.

'This does not happen often,' said the man who introduced himself as D.I. Donald. 'Two tips both pointing in the same direction.' Dick looked at him questioningly. 'I'm quite sure I was the only one in the area,' he said. 'I certainly didn't see anyone else.'

'You must understand I cannot divulge any details,' said the policeman. 'I can only confirm that your tip and the other one match perfectly. We will try to retrieve the car this morning. If everything is as you say, we should prepare ourselves for a dreadful discovery that will shock the country. But tell me, why did you actually follow him? Was there a specific reason?'

Dick decided to tell him the whole story, from the punch at the training field to the confrontation in the hotel lobby. 'I followed him on an impulse really,' he decided. 'An impulse that may well stem from the story I just told you.'

D.I. Donald just nodded. 'Did you hear about the death of the Indian player?' he asked. 'It was made public late last night.'

'Vijay Apte?' asked Dick, suddenly realizing what he had witnessed yesterday afternoon.

'Yes, Vijay Apte,' confirmed D.I. Donald. 'The Indian team coach is holding a press conference at the Hilton at 11 o'clock. I presume as a journalist you may want to be there.'

Dick felt himself turn red. 'Good suggestion,' he said. 'I'll certainly be there.'

Indian coach Dilawar Jilani was visibly perspiring. There were drops on his forehead and his yellow polo was stained at his armpits. He had a piece of paper on the table, but after reading the first line he discarded it. 'We are all in shock,' he said, wiping a tear. 'Vijay was the sweetest man on earth and a cricketer in his heart and soul.

He always gave his best. You all saw that yesterday.' He paused a moment to wipe the sweat from his brow. 'We cannot understand how and why he was so suddenly ripped from our lives,' he resumed. 'We cannot say anything with certainty about the cause of death. The doctor presumes it was a heart attack. We want to take his body back to India as soon as possible for cremation. Our captain Vinoo Ramji will accompany the body and speak on behalf of the team during the ceremony. As you may know, he and Vijay had a particularly close friendship.'

At that point, Vinoo appeared behind the table. He looked somewhat dishevelled. His otherwise carefully coiffed hair was tousled and he had not shaved. 'I want to say on behalf of the entire team that we have lost not only a teammate but also a friend,' he said in a shaking voice. 'He was just about to break through. But even if his achievements on the field were not always what he wanted them to be, he was an indispensable force in the dressing room. Someone who could lift the whole team. As Dilawar said, I will accompany Vijay's body to Mumbai. I can assure you that all the other teammates will be there in spirit.'

He got up suddenly and disappeared through a side door. Dick had wanted to ask some questions, but understood that now was neither the time nor the place to insist. He rushed out of the press conference into the lobby where he sat and typed his article at breakneck speed. *The Northern Chronicle* would not miss a thing. As he had promised D.I Donald, he made no mention of what he had witnessed that night. He had enough material to write about anyway.

Almost ten minutes after he had sent his piece, his editor-in-chief Rupert Thorpe called. 'What a great article!' he cried enthusiastically. 'You've surpassed yourself. We will open with it tomorrow—that goes without saying. I knew I had sent the right man to London.'

'Now,' Dick thought, 'strike while the iron is hot, he's like putty in my hands.'

'I have a small request,' he said, trying to sound as friendly as he could.

'Come on then,' said Rupert slightly less boisterous. 'Now that the national newspapers want you, you have a stick to hit with.'

'I would like to go to Mumbai to attend the cremation.'

The silence that followed made him fear for the worst, but instead of a polite or outright rejection, he heard a bouldering laugh. 'You've got guts,' said his editor-in-chief after he had recovered. From Allesford to Mumbai, that's quite a leap. You'll be too big for our little town soon. But before you go, write at least one top story for *The Northern Chronicle* and surprise the entire country.'

'So I can go?' said Dick like a child asking his parents' permission to go on a school trip.

'You may,' said Rupert. 'I assume you can manage everything yourself. I'm too old and too lazy to be bothered with your travel arrangements. In any event, get a good hotel, drink only boiled water or mineral water from bottles and never eat at a roadside stall. I've been to India once and after Day 1, I had a bowel infection that ruined my entire trip.'

Dick glowed with emotion. He had never been beyond Paris and now he would be almost ten thousand miles away from home. And he would fly. Until now he had always managed to avoid flying. Why? He wasn't quite sure. Maybe because of his good friend Phil who had flown exactly once. During that flight from Amsterdam to Leeds he had suffered a major anxiety attack upsetting not only his fellow passengers but also the crew. Not that he hadn't taken precautions. Suffering from the aviophobia his entire family was afflicted with, Phil had armed himself with a few sturdy tranquilizers which had hardly subdued his panic. Once he had landed safely at Schiphol, he had sworn that he would never fly again. Because thoughts of Phil had distracted him, he had not heard the last part of Rupert's speech. 'I have to get back to work now,' he heard his boss say. 'A chief editor has his duties.'

Driving up north, Dick had difficulty concentrating on the road. He forced himself to use the considerable horsepower the car had to offer sparingly. An accident was the last thing he needed now. Although he was delighted to go home, even if it was just a short whirlwind stopover, he was thrilled at the prospect of being reunited with Julie and his three boys, and at the same time he already felt a little homesick—tomorrow, or the day after, he would have to leave his beloved wife and his children again. How he would miss them!

To distract himself, he turned on the radio. Used to the awful sound of the audio system in his Fiesta, he was surprised by the full sound of this state-of-the-art installation. He listened to a live Bruce Springsteen concert for a while, but The Boss's loud rock soon started to annoy him. On the news station, he heard that Vijay Apte's body was released and would be flown to Mumbai in two days. He pulled up into the first parking spot he came upon. Looking out the car window he felt the presence of his deceased brother. 'Help me a little, Joe,' he said softly. 'Stand by me if it's necessary.'

53

Tony

TONY WAS AT HIS wit's end. Could he stay out of the line of fire? Could he, an accomplice to the disappearances of Carine and her Hyundai, ever be exonerated? He could hardly resist the incredible urge to come clean. Of course, he should have called the police immediately after Michael told him he had killed Carine. Dragging the body around, the trip to Bisham Woods, getting rid of the Hyundai—he could have spared himself the entire mess. He had gotten much too involved. What would happen to him if he told to the whole story? A few years in prison at least? Even an old episode of *Wicked Tuna*—a programme he always enjoyed immensely—could not distract him.

In fact, watching the little boats on a tuna hunt made him slightly seasick. Because he needed to hear a human voice, he called Helen. He knew it was weak to reach out to the woman he had recently ousted from his life—especially at this late hour—but he had nothing else to do. Her 'hello' sounded sleepy. Tony didn't really know what to say, 'I just wanted to hear your voice,' he said slowly. 'I don't think I treated you very nicely the last time we spoke.'

'And you're telling me now? Do you know what time it is?'

Her voice had the same old sharpness that Tony almost

enjoyed. 'You're obviously in no mood for my apologies,' he said. 'I hope you can fall sleep again.'

'Of course you know that won't happen; once awake, wide awake. Tell me what's really on your mind.'

'No, that was it,' he said. 'Sorry, I woke you. Good night.' After he disconnected, he felt like a big prick. He lay down on the bed and stared at the abstract painting next to the TV. 'Messy entity' was written on a strip of paper next to it—a striking description of his inner being.

'We have to try something personal,' Tony said when he met Allan in the Danubius lobby. "A good cliché lasts more than a day", we used to say at home, but we might not get away with that now. Has our esteemed press secretary Hugh Gray come up with something or is he too tired after all his daily hard work?' Hugh Gray's slow work pace was legendary and it was only thanks to the protection of his father-in-law, Brian Jameson—chairman of the English Cricket Board—that he had been in office for two years. 'He's outdone himself,' Allan said. 'This is the concept. Just read it.' Tony picked up the piece of paper and read:

> It is with great sadness that the English team has learned of the passing of Vijay Apte, member of the Indian cricket team. He was a gifted cricketer and a gentleman. That he died in harness makes it all the more poignant. In this sad hour our thoughts are with his teammates, family and friends. We wish them much strength.

'Not bad for Hugh,' Tony said, returning the sheet of paper to Allan. Especially that "died in the harness" bit—he will consider that quite a find. Are you going to approve this for release?'

'Yes,' Allan said absently. 'Have you seen Michael yet? I want him involved in this.'

Tony felt the blood drain from his face. There was no escaping now. 'No, not yet,' he said. 'Sorry, I have to go to my room for a while.'

Allan looked at him amazed. 'Then I'll find Hugh,' he said. 'He'll be thrilled.'

Seated on his bed, Tony knew that it would just be a matter of time before Michael's disappearance would be made public. He picked up his phone and called the number the policeman had given him. 'D.I. Donald,' sounded a tired voice after a few seconds. 'I have a lot to tell you,' Tony said. 'A lot that will clear up some of the riddles you're dealing with. It has to be in person, the information is too important to convey by phone.' He felt strangely calm, relieved that the pressure of the last days would soon be lifted.

'Where can I reach you?' D.I. Donald, suddenly alert, asked, 'Or would you rather come to the Yard?'

'I'll take a taxi,' Tony said. 'I'll be there in an hour.'

The immense glass wall and the spinning sign—NSY—impressed him. The concrete blocks and steel posts gave the building the appearance of a fort. Although he assumed that D.I. Donald would not object to him reporting half an hour early, he chose to take a walk around the building. He crossed the street and saw a man entering Clipper of the Yard, a gents' salon with an old-fashioned red-white Barber's Pole on the façade.

He considered a quick trim, but decided to continue his walk. On Broadway, he walked into a pub, a deep narrow establishment where, in better days, he could have happily spent hours. 'Keep calm and drink'—read a sign behind the bar, an advice he could definitely take to heart. From the staggering amount of beer on offer he chose a Doom Bar which he downed in a few gulps. The drink felt good and he could just barely resist the temptation to order another one. Looking at his watch, he saw he had five more minutes, enough time to report to the Yard. With a quick pace, he walked back to the glass edifice and signed in.

After he had told his story, the policeman looked at him dispassionately. 'That's quite a story indeed,' he said. 'Aiding and assisting in the disappearance of a body and a car involved in a crime.

'As I said, quite a story. I'm afraid you will have to inform your employer that you will not be available for a while.'

'That's an understatement,' thought Tony. 'You might as well say you're going to be doing porridge.'

The relief he had felt earlier had faded into a sense of despondency. He, Tony Abbott, physiotherapist of the English cricket team, was scarred for life. He looked at his hand and felt the pain swell.

54

Vinoo

IT WAS A STRANGE sensation. His dead friend was in the belly of the Jet Airways plane on his way to India. In his mind, Vinoo replayed their last chess game. Vijay had won, playing an ingenious, complicated combination. He saw Vijay's polite glee and felt his hand on his shoulder. 'Not badly played, buddy. Better luck next time.'

'Then, of course, you'll let me win,' he had answered. 'You're much too good for me.'

The beautiful chess set Vijay was so proud of was the only thing he wanted to inherit from his friend. With a smile he remembered how proud Vijay had been of the ivory pieces and the carved rim of the board. They had spent so many hours in each other's company, the game between them on a table. Vinoo felt the first few tears well up in his eyes. Because he didn't want the members of the Board of Control for Cricket in India to see him like that, he fixed his gaze on the bright blue sky.

Jet Airways, the company who had made the plane available for the flight to India and the company for which Vinoo had done a few lucrative commercials, had the patent on extremely attractive yellow-and-black uniformed flight attendants. Even though the woman who served him seemed duly unimpressed with his status as a top cricketer, she did everything she could to make him comfortable. After she had served him a tasteful looking meal which he trifled with more than ate, he tried to focus on his arrival in Mumbai. The newspaper reporters would undoubtedly be there in droves as well as the numerous radio and television stations. It would take all his self-control to get through this ordeal without too many tears.

The entire trip he had been drafting a speech in his head, but nothing had seemed right so far. Highly praising Vijay's capabilities as a cricketer would be insincere and only talking about their friendship might be too personal. To clear his mind, Vinoo tried to concentrate on an article about climate change in a newspaper that was handed to him as he boarded the plane, but he had no idea what he read. He put the newspaper on the armrest, swallowed one of the sleeping pills the Indian team doctor had given him and slowly drifted away.

In the arrival hall in Mumbai, the chaos was immediate. To escape being trampled, security officers escorted him to a room provisionally set up as a press room. It was small and cramped; a large number of journalists pressed against the walls. And there was no air conditioning. Vinoo who was still dressed in clothes apt for the English weather—when he had left London it had been barely sixty-five degrees—took off his jacket. He did not care that his shirt hung around him like a wet cloth. It was all about Vijay now. 'He was my friend,' he began, 'a friend like I will never have again.' He briefly sketched how they met a long time ago and recalled several highlights of their friendship. When he was finished, the room remained quiet.

He endured impassively the short and intense applause that followed. The questions had but one point. 'What was the cause of death? Did Vijay have a medical history?'

'Apparently a heart attack,' he said, knowing better. 'The team's press secretary will keep you informed.' He glanced at Jahangir Singh who sat next to him looking important. Jahangir had been the team's press secretary for as long as anyone could remember and had done so to everyone's satisfaction. He was vain but in a nice way. His extravagant style of dress and outlandish glasses made him the team's talisman and they all liked having him around.

The press conference was not yet over and Aasia joined him. In the last few days, she had been completely absent from his mind, but now she made sure she was in the spotlight. She hung on his arm as if it was the last available lifebuoy in a sinking ship. Vinoo hid how unpleasant he felt behind a forced smile. 'I actually had an appointment with Farhan Khan, you know my leading man, but I had to be here, of course,' she said. Vinoo nodded vaguely as he waited for the room to empty out.

'I told you he has relationship problems. I have sort of become his counsellor. He trusts me completely. Aren't you a little jealous?' She looked at him with what was undoubtedly meant to be a sultry look. Vinoo knew she was acting but did not let on. 'No, of course I'm not jealous,' he said. 'I know I can trust you. And anyway, how could I be jealous of a man six feet tall, who makes you strain your neck every time you have to kiss him?'

Aasia looked at him uncertainly. 'I shouldn't have asked you that,' she said. 'You know I love you.' But Vinoo did not know that at all. He did know there was only one woman in the world he loved and that was Deepika. Even though his nemesis Dattu Lal—who he knew lay in a deep coma he was unlikely to ever wake up from—could no longer hurt them, he had booked another room at the Vivanta Hotel where he would meet his love late in the afternoon.

But first, he had to make it clear to Aasia that he had urgent things to do alone. He chose his words carefully. If she was disappointed, she didn't show it. 'Of course, talking to Vijay's father is important,' she said. 'I completely understand, but I do hope to see you after the cremation. After that, you'll be back in England and I'll have to miss you for weeks.' Because he thought the situation required it, Vinoo took her in his arms and planted a kiss on her cheek. 'What a beautiful couple,' he heard Jahangir say behind him. Turning around, Vinoo saw the press secretary staring at him with a big smile on his face.

For Vinoo, Deepika had always been the most beautiful woman on earth, but now, as she stood there in front of him in a light blue dress shirt which showed off her beautiful frail shape, she completely took his breath away. Very slowly, almost solemnly, he lifted the dress over her head, making sure not to disturb her hair. When he entered her he experienced an ecstasy so intense it nearly led to an immediate eruption. Deepika burst out laughing. 'I knew you were crazy about me,' she said, 'but this I did not expect.' Vinoo lay next to her and slid his arm under her head. 'I'm going to divorce Aasia,' he said. 'I don't want this situation anymore. You, the third wheel, and Aasia in all the glory.' As she shrugged her shoulders, he noticed that he had touched a sensitive nerve.

'You've risen far too high for me,' she said. 'I'm just a simple girl from a low caste.'

'Mine is not much higher,' he said. 'I've just climbed up, but I do not feel in any way that I am better than you. In fact, I feel just the opposite.'

'It's so unheard of, and you can't just "climb up",' she said.

'In this big city, you can,' Vinoo said. 'And we live in Mumbai. No one cares about things like castes here.' He looked at her lying beside him and saw a sad smile on her face. 'It'll be fine,' he said, realizing the foolishness of his words.

Vijay's father had arranged for Vinoo to speak to family and friends before the cremation. As captain of the Indian team and friend of the deceased, he wanted to honour that request, no matter how difficult. After Deepika's departure, he decided to stay in the hotel room where he could be anonymous. Seated at the desk next to the TV, he worked on his speech for hours, looking for the appropriate words to say—not till after midnight was he satisfied with the result. The hours that followed were filled with clammy dreams in which Vijay's bulging eyes played the lead.

At 6 a.m., he got up, took a cold shower and shaved himself carefully. He stood in front of the window in his boxer shorts and watched the morning sun burn away the mist. It promised to be a hot day. That he would constantly be accompanied by two bodyguards gave him a calm feeling.

There were not many people standing in the scorching sun, certainly no more than fifty. Vijay's father had insisted that the cremation should not be a public spectacle. Standing in the bright light, Vinoo looked over the heads at the horizon where the heat shimmered. Though he was wearing light linen, he perspired profusely. He quickly checked for moisture spots, but he did not see any. Looking up, he saw a flash in the distance as if the sun had hit a mirror.

After a nod from Vijay's father, he walked to the lectern with a microphone and paper in hand. He was hesitant at the beginning of his speech, but gradually became more confident and no longer needed to look at his paper. Looking in to the white light, he spoke with emotion. He saw how the heads in front of him swayed back and forth as if following him in his trance. Speaking faster and faster he took them to the highest summits of a friendship that had filled his life.

'I will never experience this again,' he said. 'Vijay is irreplaceable.' He paused for a moment to let the words sink in. Birds that had so far not made a peep, as if not wanting to interrupt his speech, suddenly burst in a song of the highest praise. A sultry breeze made the heat almost bearable.

As he braced himself for his closing words, intending to make that final and lasting impact, forever locking the memory of his friend in the hearts of all those present, he heard a sharp noise crack through the air followed by a ripping pain in his right arm.

Filled with horror, he saw his right hand strangely dangle, barely connected to his arm. As the blood gushed, he tried to stop it with his left hand, but to no avail. Everyone present was stunned by the bullet impact and it took several seconds before hands grabbed him from behind the lectern and steered him to a car that pulled up with screeching tires.

The pain was almost unbearable and it took tremendous effort not to scream. 'Main artery,' he heard someone say. 'We have to be fast. He's losing a lot of blood.' Slowly, he felt the strength ebb from his body. 'Do not faint,' he thought. 'Stay alert.' But nothing could stop the blackness that steadily engulfed him.

55

Dick

Dick had not expected it to be so difficult get permission to attend Vijay Apte's cremation. 'Actually, only the big newspapers are permitted to attend,' said the volunteer. 'It's a closed, private ceremony. And I have never heard of *The Northern Chronicle*. But Dick persisted and after much back-and-forth, he finally obtained a pass. 'Try and find a spot out of sight,' the man said. 'Just stand at the back.'

It was hot. Blistering hot with not a tree in sight for shade. The light breeze that had first offered some relief had stopped blowing and the sun drilled holes in the parched earth. Peering from behind an obese man whose fat neck was pocked with acne scars and speckled with perspiration, Dick watched Vinoo Ramji pull a piece of paper from his pocket, position himself behind the lectern and then, somewhat hesitatingly, start his eulogy.

As he spoke, his hesitation faded and he was compelling and passionate. Dick physically felt Vinoo's sincere emotion take hold of the audience. The loud crack which violently interrupted Vinoo's tribute to his friend sounded like the sharp lash of a whip. Dick watched as Vinoo reached for his arm, staggered, and was then quickly whisked away from behind the lectern.

This attempt of assassination of India's superstar was clearly unexpected as no one seemed to be in charge of the situation. People ran in all directions, shouting unintelligible commands. Dick turned around and was instantly blinded by the dazzling sunlight. It took a few seconds for his eyes to adjust and focus. In the distance, he saw a shadow behind the open window of the only house in his view. On impulse and without realizing he was putting himself in danger, Dick sprinted towards the house. Sweat gushed from his pores and he felt as if the heat would suffocate him. Halfway there, he nearly tripped over a pothole.

He tried to maintain his balance as he stumbled across the final distance to the house. He was just a few dozen meters away when he saw a small man with a full-grown black beard. He had a case of some kind in his hand and he was getting into in a light blue Toyota. Dick analysed if it was a good idea to sprint after the car, but luck was on his side—there was a row of taxis waiting for the ceremony to end.

The driver he chose turned out to be perfect for the job; he agreed instantly for the chase. How he managed to keep his eye on the prey in the insane traffic was a mystery to Dick. Ignoring all traffic rules, he kept the blue Toyota in sight. His English was rudimentary but good enough to understand Dick's instructions. Somewhere near a fish market—the smell was unmistakable— the Toyota stopped. The man with the beard disappeared into a medium-sized house with a rickety, old air-conditioning installed on the balcony.

Dick asked his driver to wait. Knowing that he was in for trouble and would most certainly need help, he asked the driver for the local emergency number and the exact address of the place they were in. He called the number, explained his situation as clearly as possible to someone who did not interrupt him once and had barely finished when the bearded man exited the house, got back in the car and drove off.

Dick was unsure of what to do. Was it wise to follow him or was it sensible to leave? He chose the first. His driver was obviously enjoying the chase and drove even more recklessly than before, never losing sight of the Toyota, even in the labyrinth of tiny alleys they found themselves in.

'Never been here before,' he said. 'This neighbourhood has a bad reputation.' That seemed like an understatement—everything about the area felt dodgy. The Toyota stopped in front of a square white house. Dick instructed his driver to park a bit further down the road before he got out of the car. The heat was more intense now and the stench of decay in the air was stifling. Dick cautiously crept down the alley next to the house. There was a window but it was too high to look into. As he combed the area looking for something to stand on, he heard a door slam. He instinctively pressed himself against the wall, knowing perfectly well there was nowhere to hide. In fact, he was completely exposed—an ideal target.

His eye fell on a rusty bucket that looked like it might provide him with just enough height to reach the window. Silently, he crept to it, grabbed the handle and soundlessly positioned the bucket underneath the window. As quietly as he could, he stepped on the bucket and grabbed hold of the narrow windowsill. The room was empty.

Just as he decided to step off the bucket, someone kicked it brutally from beneath him. Desperately, he tried to cling to the windowsill, but it offered no support and he fell backwards, landing hard on his head. His skull seemed to split open and things only got worse when someone aggressively grabbed him and threw him on his stomach.

The knife on his throat brought him back to his senses. 'Get in the house,' he heard someone say, in heavily accented English, 'where I can slit your throat in peace.' His assailant seemed to have already done a bit of the job; Dick felt warm blood trickle down his neck. He was roughly pulled up and the push in his back made him teeter. Still dizzy, he walked as slowly as possible to the back of the house. He thought of Julie, he thought of Owen, Ben and Harry. And he felt sorry for himself. He, Dick Anthony, *The Northern Chronicle's* fresh, young reporter, specialising in exposing local and regional injustices, would now meet his end in some obscure Mumbai backstreet because of his own stupidity.

They had almost reached the corner of the house when Dick heard a deep sigh behind him. Almost simultaneously, the pressure of the knife on his throat was gone. 'I told you, not a good neighbourhood,' said the driver, wiping a knife on his dirty trouser leg. 'We are leaving, and fast.' After a short sprint, they reached the car. The devil in the driver emerged as they screeched on two wheels around the corner, fleeing the scene of disaster. Only then did the full impact of fear hit Dick. He wanted to throw up his intestines, but all he could produce was acid.

56

Epilogue

I<small>T WAS HECTIC AT</small> the police headquarters. In the cacophony around him, Dick occasionally picked up a few words—'fight for life', 'lot of blood loss.' He was taken to a small room where the noise was thankfully muted. The man seated in front of him was in his forties, had slick combed-back hair, a hooked nose, and introduced himself as Amir Singh.

He offered Dick a cigarette which he, a vehement non-smoker, almost accepted because he was so tense. 'Thanks to you, we have a big fish,' Singh said. 'A very big fish. A powerful man who wanted to make an example of Vinoo; to show everyone they had no choice but to go along with his corrupt practices. But with Vinoo, he chose the wrong example.' He nodded with gusto as if to give his words extra weight, lit a cigarette and puffed vigorously. 'We got there a few minutes after your call,' he continued. He inhaled deeply and then snapped his cigarette in two in an ashtray. 'Filthy habit,' he muttered, 'I've quit three times this year.'

Dick tried to sympathize with the nicotine addict in front of him, but was now burning with curiosity. Amir Singh, however, apparently felt he had said enough. He stared out of the window in silence for a while as his hand, like a magnet, unconsciously reached for his cigarettes several times. 'We found the dead man,' he finally said. 'Your driver is a good man. I would appreciate it if you stayed in Mumbai for a few days. We may need you.'

Back in his hotel room, Dick immediately turned on the TV while he tried to get Julie on the phone, succeeding on the second attempt. She had heard of the attack. 'It's big news here,' she said. 'The TV stations can't seem to get enough of it.' Dick did not mention his adventure and chatted to his wife instead about trivial affairs in Allesford. After she broke the connection, Dick focused his eyes on the screen. Because no cameras had been present at the ceremony, the TV viewers had to do with the jerky videos and images a few alert people had captured using their mobile phones.

As Dick watched the news, his true calling slowly dawned upon him—the real reason why he had wanted to be a journalist in the first place. This was not about pillorizing a corrupt contractor in Allesford, this was global news. He grabbed his trusted Moleskine notebook and took the lift to the lobby. It was pandemonium. Dick had hoped to get a few quotes but no one seemed to want to speak to him.

After a few minutes, he spotted a man sitting on his haunches, huddled in a corner. 'I need to be very careful now,' he thought. 'Before you know it, I've ruined my chances.' He put his notebook in his pocket and carefully approached the man.

'I saw him play as a child,' he said, looking teary-eyed at Dick, 'he was no more than a toddler.' He sighed deeply and seemed unable to utter another word. Dick waited patiently; a tactic which seemed to work, as after a short while the man came to life again. 'We'll never see a player like him again,' he said. 'He was better than Sachin Tendulkar. And now he may never bat again. They say his arm has been shot to pieces.'

Dick knew better than to push further. In the lift back to his room, he feverishly tried to come up with the headline that would beat all headlines but nothing came to him. Back in his room, he stood silently near the window waiting for inspiration. The scene in the street was equal to the pandemonium in the lobby, he could sense the anguish. Behind him, on the TV, he heard the anchor announce that Vinoo had died. Standing there, high on the eleventh floor, he felt the profound sigh of collective grief rise from below and engulf him. India had lost her hero.

Later that evening, after the initial shock of the day's events had subsided, he sat at the desk in the corner of his room. Picturing Vinoo at the wicket, it was as if the floodgates in his mind were suddenly wide open and the words rushed out. In less than an hour, he wrote an article of which even he—always critical of his own work—was a little proud. By now, the TV was showing the state of a bereaved nation. Images from across the country showed masses of grieving people, all with the same empty look in their eyes. The chaos of the afternoon had given way to solemn mourning. 'India has lost the shining jewel in her crown,' he heard a commentator say. 'Life here will never be the same again. The entire cricket world will never be the same.'

Dick watched the strong and serious-looking anchor cry inappropriately, wiping his streaming tears with a handkerchief. He too felt the tears burning in his eyes. He took a bottle of whisky from the minibar next to his desk, poured a glass and sat down in front of the window. The voice of the nation's president trying to comfort his people filled the room. He picked up his phone and called Julie. As soon as he heard her voice, a great calm came over him. 'It will blow over,' she said.

But no matter how much he always wanted to believe her, this time he could not.

Acknowledgements

Two authors, one book and a publisher thousands of miles away, in New Delhi. This might not sound like a match made in heaven, but it did not deter Rupa Publications and in particular Editorial Director Dibakar Ghosh from bringing this book to life. Without Dibakar Ghosh and Editor Aparna Kumar, their enthusiasm and tireless support, this cricket thriller would never have been published.

We would like to thank the coaches on the bench—Alex de la Mar (international cricket), Nienke Oppedijk van Veen (legal advisor), Rob Oudshoorn, Marijke Bezems, Annemieke Steures, Antoinette van Riel (toxicologist, University Hospital Utrecht), Tim Bouquet (author), Harpreet Singh (Indian cricketer), Rick Hastie and Mary Godbeer (ECB), and Michael Hunt (groundsman at Lord's).

We would also like to thank Nelleke Bezems for the translation.